NARCISSISM
&
PHILANTHROPY

IDEAS AND TALENT DENIED

Gerald Freund

VIKING

VIKING
Published by the Penguin Group
Penguin Books USA Inc., 375 Hudson Street,
New York, New York 10014, U.S.A.
Penguin Books Ltd, 27 Wrights Lane,
London W8 5TZ, England
Penguin Books Australia Ltd, Ringwood,
Victoria, Australia
Penguin Books Canada Ltd, 10 Alcorn Avenue,
Toronto, Ontario, Canada M4V 3B2
Penguin Books (N.Z.) Ltd, 182–190 Wairau Road,
Auckland 10, New Zealand

Penguin Books Ltd, Registered Offices:
Harmondsworth, Middlesex, England

First published in 1996 by Viking Penguin,
a division of Penguin Books USA Inc.

10 9 8 7 6 5 4 3 2 1

LIBRARY OF CONGRESS CATALOGING-IN-PUBLICATION DATA
Freund, Gerald, 1930–
Narcissism and philanthropy : ideas and talent denied / Gerald Freund.
p. cm.
ISBN 0–670–86468–4 (alk. paper)
1. Endowments—United States. 2. Endowment of research—United States.
3. Gifted persons—Scholarships, fellowships, etc.—United States. I.Title.
HV91.F685   1996
361.7'0973—dc20   96–12911

This book is printed on acid-free paper. ∞

Printed in the United States of America
Set in Stempel Garamond
Designed by Junie Lee

To my wife, Peregrine—
and to my sons Jonathan, Matthew, Andrew

ACKNOWLEDGMENTS

First and foremost, I thank my friend Bobbie Bristol without whose editorial help and revisions this book could not have been published. I also wish to thank Margaret Mahoney, President Emeritus of the Commonwealth Fund, who has long encouraged this study as has F. Champion Ward, formerly Vice President of the Ford Foundation and a colleague at the John T. and Catherine D. MacArthur Foundation. Kenneth W. Thompson was a significant influence during my formative foundation years at the Rockefeller Foundation and since then. My friend William Plowden and I co-chaired a seminar on major foundation issues in 1991–92 which was backed by the late Robert N. Kreidler of the Dana Foundation, also by the John Merck Fund thanks to Olivia Hatch Farr and Robert M. Pennoyer, and by the Ford Foundation where the late Edward J. Mead, Jr. took a special interest in issues of foundation support of exceptionally talented individuals. Margo Viscusi and Richard H. Nolte were among the seminar's most thoughtful contributors, and their ideas influenced mine. Valuable research support was provided by Sarah E. Meyer, Anne Matthews of Princeton University, and Joseph R. Bookmyer of The Rockefeller Foundation. Elisabeth Hegarty gave expert and indefatigable secretarial assistance throughout. I am grateful to my friend Peter Mayer of Viking/Penguin for his faith in the book. Robert Dreesen at Viking/Penguin, Adrian Nicole LeBlanc, and especially my colleague at Private Funding Associates, Katherine Macaulay, made many helpful editing and other suggestions. I am very grateful to Emily Mandelstam for her ideas and for giving moral support when it was most needed.

CONTENTS

PREFACE

This book was written with great respect for the historic achievements of American foundations and the contributions generations of their professional officers have made to American and world society. The work stems from my concern for foundations' priorities over the last two decades and where these priorities are taking them today. My discussion of the evolving foundation scene is not an attempt to be a comprehensive assessment of this diverse field (there are more than forty thousand foundations of different types: private independent, operating, corporate, and community). Nor is this a foundation history; many books provide the historical overview. Instead, my focus is on the important issues confronting foundations and how their diverse missions have been carried out, with special emphasis on the priority that foundations have historically assigned to discovering, recognizing, and nurturing uniquely talented individuals and bringing them to prominence in their fields. My analysis aims to uncover what has happened to that priority in recent years and what accounts for the changes.

The stakes are high: The responsibility foundations have as participants in social and intellectual processes is significant. Foundations occupy a unique station in society, being different from other players by virtue of their ability to exert influence how and when they choose. Their independent human and financial resources can have enormous impact, belying their actual size. Foundations have the muscle to make far-reaching, creative demonstrations as well as to bring about actual changes. How they exercise power—their vision, priorities, objectives, and methods—matters greatly.

Contemporary foundations generally do not have strong institutional memories. It is useful to recall some of their most important achievements of the past lest they become totally obscured. Like new leadership of other institutions, every new generation of foundation leaders insist on making its mark, partly by distinguishing itself from predecessors. In the leaders' preoccupation with the contemporary world, past accomplishments and the lessons that can be drawn from them are perhaps being ignored. In any event, scant attention is given to what their forerunners achieved, to their vision and how they realized it, to the significance of their successes and failures. Unfortunately, history ignored or forgotten is history rewritten.

Foundations do not take kindly to outsiders' criticism; nor do they receive much, apart from that of occasional congressional investigators—and they have not drawn serious blood for a long time. Effective self-criticism from foundation ranks is rare. Commissions come and go, leaving little behind them except pounds of paper. Critical articles, whether by insiders or by outsiders, are not welcome and are rarely published. The foundation community has retributive power, which acts as a chilling deterrent to anyone with aspirations to receiving support. For example, when the anthropologist Teresa J. Oldendahl published her 1990 scholarly book challenging the conventional wisdom about the giving habits among the "philanthropic elite," she instantly felt the wrath of foundation orthodoxy. There were walkouts when she presented papers and she was told a priori that she would not get foundation support for future scholarship.

In the past, applications for support by researchers on foundations were regularly turned down. Presently, inquiries to foundations for support of research on foundations or the nonprofit sector are regularly directed to the Aspen Institute's Nonprofit

Sector Research Fund, created and controlled by a group of foundations. Research centers in the field—including the best of them, like Yale University's Program on Non-Profit Organizations—must themselves regularly apply to foundations for support. Even senior foundation scholars may be slapped down if they are perceived to be out of line. Waldemar A. Nielsen, a former foundation officer and a seasoned observer of foundations, wrote in a balanced appraisal in the journal *Chronicle of Philanthropy* that the retiring president of the Ford Foundation had failed to be a creative leader, an opinion that was shared by others though hitherto unpublished. The article, though complimentary on other grounds, provoked attacks on Nielsen in a storm of defensive letters to the *Chronicle.* The foundation drawbridge is always in position to be pulled up, its archers ready to man the battlements of orthodoxy as soon as dissent threatens to breach official lines.

I spent forty years in the academic world, arts and public affairs organizations, and foundations. For nine years I was a social science, humanities, and arts officer of the Rockefeller Foundation; in the initial years of the John D. and Catherine T. MacArthur's Prize Fellows Program, I was first a development consultant, then a vice president organizing and administering its program; I have headed the Whiting Foundation's Writers Awards since its inception in 1984. I also organized the Lila Wallace–Reader's Digest Fund's Writers Program and have created and administered programs at other major foundations and for family funds and individual trusts. I participated in the creation of major projects during that time. But the common denominator and my most significant foundation experience has been to identify and nurture talented individuals. For many years, that was also a mainstream activity of major foundations and the key to their success in defining the problems on which they then unleashed those exceptionally qualified to solve or at least mitigate them. My analysis aims to show how this priority has given way to an ingrown, narcissistic tendency at many foundations.

From my experience in the world of philanthropy, I have drawn conclusions regarding how foundations and their officers can work most effectively and successfully. My most urgent recommendation is for the restoration of active searches for exceptional talent—making them the centerpiece of foundation programs—and for giving priority to the support of activities that have such talent at their helm.

NARCISSISM

PHILANTHROPY

1

MODERN PHILANTHROPY AND EXCEPTIONAL INDIVIDUALS

Foundations are a mystery to most people. The general public, lacking a good understanding of what their purposes are or even what they have achieved, fail to appreciate what they are able to accomplish for the benefit of society. Foundations are most known for their sponsorship of public television programs and the underwriting of local sports teams and cultural events. But that is a very thin end of the wedge, both of what foundations do and of what they are capable of doing.

What is a foundation? It is a not-for-profit organization having a principal fund of its own, managed by its own trustees or directors, and established to maintain or assist educational, social, charitable, religious, artistic, scientific, or other activities that serve the common welfare. Foundations exist in other countries but are especially prominent in the United States, where Congress, to stimulate giving, provided for tax deductibility of contributions to foundations as to other charities. Foundation policies and practices here receive close attention, partly because of public fascination with wealth and the way it is used, and also because foundation grants may set important new trends.

In the eighteenth and nineteenth centuries, foundations were conceived to perform "charitable work" that government did not and was not expected to do. By the middle of the twentieth century, foundations were at the very center of exchanges of information about social problems and emerging ideas. This gave them a powerful, central place in the growing, vast nonprofit sector of society.

By their actions, foundations may affect individual institutions or a whole class of them, specific projects or whole fields of research. They may play a key role in the vitality of art forms and of new social movements. They are therefore instruments of innovation and social adaptation that are more influential than other agencies. Above all, foundations are able to identify complex issues of policy and public affairs and match them with those who are most competent to deal with them. While all foundations have some influence, the largest of them have the funds to give them a potential leverage beyond any other kind of institution in the nonprofit sector and often rivaling the major for-profit private institutions.

According to 1993 Internal Revenue Service figures, 20 percent of 41,348 foundations had $162 billion or 91 percent of foundation assets and gave about $9 billion a year in grants. Quantitatively, foundation giving is less important than individual giving: foundation support amounts to only about 9 percent of the total funds generous Americans contribute philanthropically and charitably every year. But foundation money is the most precious of these dollars, for it is available to be invested dynamically—that is, to solve our toughest ongoing problems: scarce resources, hunger, disease, domestic violence, warfare among and within nations, ignorance, destruction of cultural values, racism.

Endowments of the largest private independent foundations, which have names like Ford, Rockefeller, Mellon, Johnson, and MacArthur, are generally derived from a single source, such as a family. Decisions are generally made by an independent board of directors or trustees, although a bank or trust officer may act on the donor's behalf. Most larger independent foundations have staff, usually referred to as officers or administrators, who are responsible for carrying out the foundation's policies and programs.

There are three other categories of foundations:

- Company-sponsored foundations, whose funds derive from profit-making businesses. Their giving tends to be in fields related to corporate activities or in communities where the sponsoring corporations operate.
- Operating foundations, which use their resources to conduct research or provide a service. They make few if any grants.
- Community foundations, publicly sponsored, whose assets are made up of contributions received from many donors. Grant decisions are made by a board of directors and are generally limited to local charitable organizations.

While foundations in these categories make important contributions of many kinds, especially in community development and support, private independent foundations have taken the most significant initiatives toward creative changes; they make the most of philanthropic venture capital. Their funds have been used most effectively when focused on finding gifted individuals with potentially innovative approaches to intractable problems. As important as this has turned out to be, such direct support was not given until long after the first large foundations were created and, as we will see, may be an endangered practice today.

In recent years, public attention has been distracted from foundation missions by scandals at United Way and, especially, at the Foundation for New Era Philanthropy, the Philadelphia-based scam to which wealthy people gave money when they were promised it would be doubled with funds from anonymous phil-anthropists. Additional media attention has been monopolized by the two national foundations, the National Endowment for the Arts and the companion National Endowment for the Humani-ties. The Endowments' budgets are small but their funds come from taxpayers. That has precipitated attacks from conservative congressmen and the Christian Right, who oppose supporting any artist and humanist with the argument that their endeavors are the extremist experiments of a few.

Foundations have often been seen, especially by those who disagree with their missions, as "liberal" or as serving a liberal agenda. Indeed, in the hostile propaganda of the right, founda-tions have been held responsible for all manner of sins and social diseases—from Darwinism to women's right to choose, sex edu-cation for children, opportunities for minorities, and public mani-festations of "alien" cultures. The truth is, most foundations tend to follow rather than lead when it comes to ideas of social, eco-nomic, or political change. Unfortunately, the intensity of the conservative onslaught has driven some foundations into narrow, "politically correct" agendas, which add grist to the propaganda mill.

There have always been major foundations that have been dis-tinctly conservative in their programs and practices. In recent years, however, the numbers and assets of new right-of-center foundations and politically conservative think tanks have multi-plied. These foundations have become bold in exercising power, teetering at the edge of the kind of overt political lobbying that they have perennially accused liberal foundations of doing. Their arrival on the scene has led the foundation field to feel that it has a new source of protection against congressional hostility, because the leadership of the conservative foundations, such as Bradley and Olin, may help to ward off attacks and to resist legislative efforts to encroach on the autonomy of foundations. How this will play itself out in Congress remains to be seen.

All but obscured by these controversies is the astonishing growth in recent years in the number of foundations funded by the riches of the Reagan-Bush era, as well as a surge in planned giving that includes the creation of trusts and foundations.

Established foundations have also experienced remarkable growth. At the beginning of 1994, the Ford Foundation had $6.75 billion in assets and the W. K. Kellogg Foundation $6.5 billion; the Robert Wood Johnson, the Pew Charitable Trusts, and five others each reached more than $2 billion; and another ninety-one foundations had assets of over $220 million apiece. In addition, over the course of the next decade or so, there will occur a wealth transfer of unprecedented proportions—in the trillions of dollars—from the senior generation, giving rise to many new foundations and charitable trusts. Although it is possible that Congress will attempt to impose new taxes or regulations on the burgeoning philanthropic institutions, their numbers will increase and some will have assets equaling those of the largest foundations. Escalating assets and new sources of funds will offer opportunities to foundations whose trustees and personnel staff have the vision to make effective use of their funds.

Foundations are growing in prominence in American society because they are increasing in number and available assets and because of their predictable impact on segments of the population and the country's institutions. What is not predictable—and this is my principal subject of discussion here—is whether foundations will mount effective programs to deal with the country's critical problems: disease, poverty and growing gap between rich and poor, cultural insensitivity, declining education standards and the degeneration of the urban public school systems, eroding family allegiances, violence and self-destruction among youth, confused values, the lack of effective leadership in every sphere of social, political, and economic life, and our global drift toward ecological suicide. A pervasive problem is that "people in general in this country," as Saul Bellow has pointed out, "have lost the habit of debating questions. . . . Where there is free speech without any debate, what you have is a corruption of free speech, which very quickly becomes demagogy."

To define our society's key problems and point to solutions takes leadership by the most talented among us. In the past, foundations gave highest priority to discovering, supporting, and elevating to prominence generations of exceptionally talented individuals, who could bring their talents to bear on key issues. The success of such partnerships between foundations and creative thinkers and practitioners has resulted in some far-reaching innovations in our culture, such as the eradication of hookworm by Charles W. Stiles (with the support of the Rockefeller Foundation); the creation of the New York City Ballet and its school by George Balanchine (Ford Foundation); the development of highly productive corn plants by Norman Borlaug (Rockefeller Foundation); and the provocative investigation of race problems in democracy by Gunnar Myrdal in 1962 (Carnegie Corporation). These undertakings were guided by exceptionally talented individuals, without whom they could not have been launched, let alone brought to fruition, but it was the foundations that identified the right leadership, helped to define their undertakings, and intervened at a critical moment with financial support. Principal officers and their program staff (as well as trustees) invariably knew highly qualified people to consult and recruit for the success of significant ventures. Their knowledge grew out of the training and experience they had before joining foundations, as well as their continued involvement with the intellectual and scientific leadership of the time.

Foundations that were most active in grantmaking, such as Rockefeller, Carnegie, Ford, Johnson, and Sloan, had major programs supporting individual scholarship and the scientific work of those who were best qualified to lead major activities and advise the foundations on priorities. Networks of such talent, developed over many years, continually worked with foundations. The ties that were created between foundation administrators and the day's principal thinkers and practitioners gave foundations access to the right people to consult and recruit for the success of significant ventures. Such interrelationships with excellence are at least as important to foundation missions today.

Instead, in many fields, former networks are eroding. There are fewer interchanges with top minds, especially in the social sciences and humanities; fewer in-depth relationships with academics, research institutes, and major government offices. Former collaborators note that the new generation of program officers is not interested in outside opinion about their priorities and programs. Experts in a certain field often feel excluded from foundation counsels. Increasingly, foundations seem to prefer to go it alone or to talk only to those outsiders who will conform to what has already been decided.

These major changes are transforming the place foundations occupy and the way they attempt to use their power and influence. Prominent scholars and practitioners are sufficiently concerned about these changes to have spoken out critically. The internationally renowned environmental scholar Gilbert F. White, in an address to the American Philosophical Society, said: "During the last few years one trend in private foundation policy deserving of critical review is the setting of moderately explicit priority programs which funding applicants must address if they are to expect sympathetic response. This is in contrast to a more traditional stance of inviting ideas circumscribed only by very broad subject boundaries. To the extent this trend discourages innovative, unconventional ideas, it may work against exploration of problems for which society has little precedent."

From a different vantage point, the artistic director and critic Robert Brustein sees "a lockstep mentality ruling today's funding fashions," while Pablo Eisenberg, cochair of the National Committee for Responsive Philanthropy, ascribes "the enormous communications gap between donors and grant recipients" to "the arrogance of many philanthropic institutions and their cavalier treatment of grantees and would-be grantees."

Seen in the context of the evolution of modern philanthropy, the foundation "closed shop" is the return of a narcissistic trend that had its origin with Andrew Carnegie eighty-five years ago.

The era of modern philanthropy began at the turn of this century, when the first large foundations were created with endowments that were treated as venture capital for the promotion of the common good. This contrasted with conventional charity practiced up to that time, motivated in America by Christian doctrine and the Puritan ethic. The rich, or those just better off, sought to enter heaven by giving generously to oppose the infirmities, misfortunes, and vices of others. Until about the middle of the nineteenth century, charity in the United States was largely motivated by communal and class interests, which paralleled ongoing personal and ecclesiastical concerns. Still, charitable practice did not focus on the individual recipient until around the end of the nineteenth century. It was not until long after the arrival of Andrew Carnegie and John D. Rockefeller that individuals began to receive genuine support. Carnegie and Rockefeller were the leading nonprofit venture capitalists, whose charitable contributions were based on their immense personal fortunes. Their approaches were very different.

In creating a foundation and other philanthropic institutions, Carnegie had something other than charity in mind. He declared: "Neither the individual nor the race is improved by almsgiving." As a follower of Herbert Spencer's Social Darwinism, Carnegie rationalized a hands-off attitude toward all social problems. But he believed that rich men had a responsibility for good works: "The man who dies thus rich dies disgraced." He threw himself into philanthropy with an enthusiasm equal to a revivalist's fervor. Carnegie's Social Darwinism led naturally to his imposing his private vision of the public good. Giving hundreds of thousands and millions of dollars, he set conditions recipients had to meet to qualify for support; meanwhile, he passed himself off as a sage. His narcissistic approach led to some disastrous consequences, such as his choice, as an officer of the Carnegie Corporation, of Charles B. Davenport, who propagated the doctrine of eugenics, used to justify racism in America. Carnegie, supremely convinced of his superior wisdom, experience, and ability, created institutions when he could not find a vehicle to serve his purpose. He was sure he was better able to do for the poor "than they would or could do for themselves" and left a very personal stamp on all the philanthropies he created. The Carnegie Corporation was his headquarters and became his residuary legatee. He created the Carnegie Foundation for the Advancement of Teaching, the Carnegie Institute of Pittsburgh, the Carnegie Institution of Washington. Perhaps the best known of his institutional creations were the Carnegie Endowment for International Peace and the public library system he endowed with unparalleled generosity. (He also built the Peace Palace at The Hague and endowed universities in the British Isles.) In initiating these many institutions, he listened mainly and sometimes only to himself; he was the originator of and epitome of the narcissistic tradition in American philanthropy.

John D. Rockefeller was a great admirer of Carnegie and told him so. But Rockefeller followed a very different path in guaranteeing that he would be able to pass through the eye of a needle to enter heaven. A devout Christian, a tithing Baptist all his adult life, he gave charitably to education, missionary work, and other needs of the poor and the sick. But Rockefeller also differed from

Carnegie in that he listened to others, foremost to educators, theologians, public officials; he studied the ideas and plans presented to him for significant betterment of the society. Already in 1889, he made his first major contribution to the creation of the University of Chicago, a great midwestern "citadel of learning."

Rockefeller's philanthropies were directed by hardheaded evaluations of proposals brought to him by others. He had a knack for picking talented associates and ensuring their loyalty, beginning in 1891 with the appointment of Frederick Taylor Gates, who helped organize all of Rockefeller's benefactions. Gates was the first in a long line of associates who made sure that the most objective, even selfless, philanthropic decisions were made. He called it "scientific giving"—giving directed by the head rather than by the ego, as in Carnegie's solo flights of self-adduced munificence. Rockefeller's ideas and strategies were based on the advice of experts and, like Carnegie's, had next to nothing in common with almsgiving. But unlike Carnegie's narcissistic system, this was the beginning of a tradition whereby opportunities for creativity were given with conviction on the part of those who served as agents of the Rockefeller family. That conviction was passed along to those who were its beneficiaries. Succeeding generations of Rockefellers recruited the best brains they could attract to investigate competing clams on their philanthropies. They looked for well-educated advisers who were idealistic professionals, individuals with ideas and a talent for rigorous analysis and keen evaluation. Most were inveterate learners who had a thirst for knowledge of all kinds. The principal advisers were themselves accomplished in one profession or field, having earned the respect of their peers as scientists or scholars.

Rockefeller's recruitment standards and practices of advised philanthropy influenced other foundations. This was especially noticeable in the decades following World War II, when major new foundations were created, such as Ford and Johnson, and existing ones were expanded. Overall, the narcissistic approach to philanthropic policy choices and decisionmaking was not influential in the practices of new foundations through the 1930s and 1940s, and it finally lost its hold even on Carnegie's philanthropic enterprises.

Gerald Jones, in *The Circuit Riders,* his book on the Rockefeller Foundation, concluded it was "Rockefeller's essentially impersonal gospel of wealth, rather than Carnegie's self-aggrandizing model, that became the norm in the new century." But narcissistic, centrist philanthropy has since made a major comeback, spreading its influence to foundations both large and small, as we shall see.

The late John E. Sawyer, president of Williams College and then of the Andrew W. Mellon Foundation, warned that there is an unhealthy atmosphere in foundations when interest in serious debate is lacking and no equivalent of academic freedom exists. "My experience as a college president in the late 1960s and as a foundation officer a decade later stands in striking contrast—the former was challenged on almost any issue, even when right, the latter was seldom interrupted, even when wrong." Sawyer learned that a foundation can get its bearings in a field only by enlisting a network of reliable advisers and listening attentively to them. In extended remarks, he called for heightened sensitivity on all sides of a foundation's relationships. Sawyer pointed out that organized grantmaking is an anomaly within a market-oriented economy in which money or goods of approximately equal value are normally traded. He quoted political scientist Kenneth Boulding, calling grantmaking "the one-way transfer of purchasing power," and then continued: "Operationally this one-way transfer, or the prospect of it, creates an imbalance in the relationship of the parties which all must recognize and hold under conscious control if some of the less attractive, more manipulative or oppressive sides of human interactions are to be avoided."

Sawyer believed that foundations are responsible for defining and promulgating their principal program areas; for establishing internal and external operating procedures that are comprehensible—and helpful—to those they seek to assist; and for conducting grantmaking in ways that address critical goals "on a scale and with a predictability" that can make a lasting difference.

Foundations have more to give than money. A grantee—especially the individual grantee and most particularly the young developing scientist, artist, or scholar—gets the maximum benefit from nurturing support and an ongoing relationship with a mature foundation officer who has at least a working familiarity with the grantee's field or discipline. This way, too, program administrators take the most satisfaction from the work of their grantees. The best administrators are helpful when called upon but not intrusive or prying; they do not make grantees feel they need to express inordinate or inappropriate gratitude.

In the end, it is not a foundation's money that matters most; rather, it is its ability to marshal information, identify the problems to which it should give priority, and harness and inspire the best talent to work on these problems. Foundations have a leadership role to play in organizing resources of all kinds for significant selfless purposes and for joining the most significant talents they can find to critical issues in society.

Waldemar Nielsen, a leading commentator on the not-for-profit scene, does not see that foundations recently have made identifiable breakthroughs, or a "detectable dent," in any of society's huge problems and perceives a lack of "strong and innovative leadership." He has pointed out that it is important to look closely at the grantmaking of foundations to see whether it is as targeted and strategic as they claim. He asks further if these claims "are merely hopes and intentions, or worse, just self-gratifying and propagandistic descriptions of what foundations are doing."

Giving away money is simple; nothing is easier. Giving

money away well is very hard; nothing is more difficult. Therefore, the bottom line of philanthropy is a tougher master than the businessman's bottom line. It follows that organized philanthropy, if conducted in a truly professional manner, is one of the most difficult of jobs. It entails many agonizing choices.

The common element of all charitable purposes is their designation to accomplish objectives that are beneficial to the community. There is, however, a fundamental distinction between charity and philanthropy. Funds used for life's essentials, such as food, clothing, shelter, health care, family emergencies, are classified as charity. This is almsgiving, as Andrew Carnegie called it—moneys given to improve a situation or sustain a condition but that ordinarily have no direct creative purpose. Charity represents Americans' generosity in contributing to make those less fortunate better off. It represents approximately 90 percent of voluntary giving.

Philanthropy is distinguished from charity because it has a creative edge. Its purpose is to produce something that does not already exist or to enhance through special recognition and change something that does. Philanthropy supports a vast spectrum of activity; it has unlimited horizons: a book based on research, a volume of poems, philosophic speculation, laboratory experiments, field research leading to practical solutions of problems, such as disease-resistant crop strains. Whatever the arena, the goal of philanthropic support is to unleash and extol creativity and talent.

If it were simply a matter of giving money to willing recipients, the task of a foundation officer would be much less difficult than, say, deciding what nag's nose to put bets on at the races. But if the funds are to be used to serve the interests of the maximum number of individuals, directed to most important immediate and long-term problems, then the decisions as to where to place these limited funds requires thoughtful deliberation. The range of choices is potentially infinite. Who are the few to whom you say "yes"? How much information should foundation officers have to justify a confident "yes" while saying "no" to numerous compelling claims on the same funds?

Foundations can be extraordinarily influential. They enjoy exceptional independence and so can play a unique role if they have the vision and willingness to do so. They can support what is significant but out of favor. Above all, they can dare to step in where others find the same opportunity politically untouchable. They can set out to find first-class talent and resolve to nurture it. Historically, foundations had mature and knowledgeable officers who were given the means to develop and sustain our future scientists and decisionmakers. The nurturing role may be the most important any foundation can play.

Foundations have that unusual potential if they have the right personnel. They are mostly independent of government, comparable to but differently chartered from educational institutions, and not beholden to stockholders. Though their assets may be as great as those of many corporations, the largest foundations, especially, have unique viability. Their potential for effective action is that of an adventurous venture capital business.

Finding the best and boosting them is an American tradition. We are a country of winners and losers, successes and failures, victors and vanquished. It is terribly important to us to know who is on top or in contention; to docket national heroes and goats, idols and villains; to identify lame ducks and rookies, naturals and late bloomers. Although few Americans know who Adam Smith was, or what he stood for, most Americans believe firmly, even passionately, in competition. A vital purpose of competition is to spotlight the talented, the very best individuals. Enabling such citizens to achieve their potential—for their own sakes and for the greater good they can contribute to community, state, and nation—is crucial to a changing society, especially in the United

States, with its many unsolved problems and the growing disparity between haves and have-nots. Our intellectual and creative elite are our most important resources. Spotting the imaginative minority, as Arnold Toynbee observed in 1964, "is all-important, because the outstanding creative ability of a fairly small percentage of the population is mankind's ultimate capital asset. . . . The work of creative spirits is what gives society a chance of directing its inevitable movement along constructive instead of destructive lines."

Not nearly enough efforts are made in America to spot the creative spirit in gifted children, young adults, or unrecognized older individuals. When talent is identified, there is often insufficient thought or effort given to the best ways of providing encouragement, timely assistance, and follow-through to develop its potential. Exceptions occur most frequently in science and business—professions in which invention and innovation are intimately linked with material gain—as in the corporate think tanks created by Bell Labs and 3M. Perhaps that is part of the answer. From the standpoint of this urgent need, the argument that a meritocracy exists seems academic. "Enough of the formal structure of meritocracy is in place by now," writes Nicholas Lemann, "that the educational system is the *de facto* provider of individual opportunity in America." If true, whatever it provides does not adequately serve the causes of leadership, exceptional erudition, or the gift to write moving poems or novels or enduring musical compositions.

Suspicion of the exceptional is nothing new in American society. Anti-intellectualism, distrust of scholars, and reverence for the average is evident throughout American history. In the 1830s, Alexis de Tocqueville observed the low levels of interest in education and intellect in America. One hundred thirty years later, President Lyndon B. Johnson commissioned F. Champion Ward to make a report on "Talent Development in the U.S." but disregarded the commission's findings and recommendations, chief of which was to stop neglecting our best minds, which was particularly evident among minorities. The report proposed making a major effort to seek out those unusual individuals whose passionate creativity can "advance our common life more than a thousand others of the same age, education and ambition."

Among us are men and women with extraordinary talent in every field of endeavor—business or philosophy, literature and art, statecraft, education, religion. Each of these fields has thousands of able practitioners who can enhance our survival and enrich the culture. But as the report to President Johnson indicated, in each field there are also some—and a few in the wings—who have the capacity to go beyond the reach of the normal competent individual. Yet it is probable that we are losing at least as many of these brilliant men and women as we recognize, and we encourage very few of them with support. Our educational systems do not alone deserve the blame for this failure; nor is the failure only at the school level. In the United States, we celebrate those who have made it more than we do the striving of exceptional individuals on their way up. We praise their struggle only when they have triumphed. Horatio Alger stories would not be told if the hero had not come out on top. As the report to Johnson states: "When the cure for cancer is discovered, it is likely that it could have been discovered five years earlier, if the United States had had better ways of identifying as children those humans with exceptional ability" and had given them special attention. Why not? "Intellect in America," the historian Richard Hofstadter wrote, "is resented as a kind of excellence, as a claim to distinction, as a challenge to egalitarianism."

Forbes magazine reported that state and local expenditures aimed at gifted and talented students in 1990 amounted to two cents out of every $100 appropriated to the schools. The federal Jacob K. Javits Gifted and Talented Students Act of 1988 received under $10 million in 1992, less than 0.1 percent of federal elementary and secondary funding. It is especially targeted for gifted and talented students who are economically disadvantaged, speak limited English, or have disabilities. In 1995, House Speaker Newt Gingrich's insurgents sought to cut the program so much as to virtually eliminate it.

Why should this be? Consider the minefields of language, politics, and power any program to aid talented Americans must negotiate. Despite society's preoccupation with ranking individuals, Americans remain uncomfortable with the idea of selecting superiority. The process seems to run inherently counter to their understanding of the democratic ideals of inclusiveness and equality. The "aristocracy of virtue and talent" idealized by Thomas Jefferson is either beyond general understanding or is regarded by many as a threat. Arnold Toynbee observed a generation ago that Americans have "this perverse notion that to have been born with an exceptionally large endowment of innate ability is tantamount to having committed a large pre-natal offense against society. It is looked upon as being an offense because, according to this wrong-headed view of democracy, inequalities of any kind are undemocratic. The gifted child is an offender." The righteous forces trumpeting egalitarianism will not contemplate recognizing an intellectual elite at any age.

This ostrichlike attitude notwithstanding, there are, in every form of human endeavor, individuals who excel more than others, who are endowed with a capacity to advance our common life more than the collective energy of others of the same age, education, and ambition. They are our natural elites; learning will only add to their power. Champion Ward, a wise veteran of the foundation community, points out that "Humankind had watched lightning for thousands of years before it occurred to one of them to walk out into the rainy night with the absurd intention of flying a kite. A society should keep its eyes peeled for Ben

Franklins," Ward argued, "to make sure it does not lose even one."

Modern philanthropy was under way for decades before it recognized the genius of the Franklins among us and supported them. Many years were to pass before even Rockefeller's philanthropies were to single out exceptionally gifted individuals for direct support. In the English-speaking world, such activity was pioneered by Britain's Royal Society, which used government funds as early as the 1870s to support research by individual scientists. In the United States, World War I was a great stimulus to scientific research, as war always is. The National Research Council, the arm of the National Academy of Sciences, administered science research. In 1919, the Rockefeller Foundation gave $500,000 to the National Research Council for postdoctoral fellowships in the sciences—the first major private foundation support of individuals in the United States. Although given indirectly, the grant offered support of research by independent professional scientists. In 1923, Rockefeller's new International Education Board awarded fellowship grants to a few leading European scientists, Niels Bohr among them, as well as to young scientists.

Science patronage continued to lead the way. It was again the Rockefeller Foundation that first put carefully selected professionals in charge of dispensing money to professionals. The appointment in 1932 of Warren Weaver, a distinguished scientist, to direct the foundation's science programs was to lead to an unprecedented worldwide mission to find and support the most outstanding scientific talent. This effort outlasted Weaver's twenty-seven years as director. Tracing the science talent search, Gerald Jonas's *The Circuit Riders* bears out just why Warren Weaver was an ideal leader for this enterprise. He delighted in exactitude but also had "high tolerance for uncertainty." He de-

manded all the evidence to be gathered but realized that a foundation officer is often called upon to make a decision on less evidence than he or she would like. Weaver was a remarkably
intuitive and successful gambler on talent. He consciously paved
the way for foundation leadership in discovering and supporting
the gifted, not only in the sciences but eventually also in the humanities, the social sciences, and finally the arts. But talent
searches for individuals in nonscience fields lagged far behind,
with the single exception of the John Simon Guggenheim Memorial Foundation, which began giving direct support to individuals
in the liberal arts and sciences in 1925.

Today, once again, the odds on discovering contemporary
Benjamin Franklins are longer than they ought to be. Moreover,
once we identify the especially talented among us, we feel the need
to "mainline" them—we put very bright children in classes with
slow learners in the misplaced notion of equality in action. The
goal, after all, should be excellence and not egalitarianism. Too
often these days, foundations—perhaps like schools and government officials—get matters backward. They, too, pursue egalitarianism at the expense of excellence, access at the expense of quality.
Thirty years ago, John W. Gardner, an authority on philanthropy,
urged that a balance be struck between "pure meritocracy and a
pure insistence on equality." Carried to an extreme, egalitarianism, he pointed out, leads to a rejection of standards and a tolerance for mediocrity.

But for historians such as Kathleen D. McCarthy, changes in
foundation personnel over the last thirty years are the result of the
"democratization" of foundations as they moved from "elitism to
cultural pluralism." McCarthy writes that the mid-1960s marked a
"fundamental shift from an abiding faith in the neutrality and fairness of 'disinterested' professionals to a new emphasis on what
might be termed 'self-interested expertise.' " By 1965, according

to McCarthy, "elite ideals" gave way to "democratization programs" that include "new idioms of gender, ethnicity and race."

All this happened, but not during the watch of program officers in the arts, humanities, and social sciences at major foundations throughout the 1960s. At the Rockefeller Foundation, for example (where I was an officer during those years), we found no incompatibility between funding arts programs and funding women and minority artists. Such foundations as Danforth, Carnegie, Ford, Rockefeller, mounted programs to search out minority talent to develop in a number of fields. All candidates were subjected to high standards of excellence, which were maintained throughout the 1960s. It was the post-sixties generation of administrators in the arts and other disciplines in public and private grantmaking who replaced objective evaluation and rigorous standards at major foundations in order to achieve the often preconceived political ends McCarthy describes with their allocations in the arts and in other fields.

While equality of opportunity is a goal—especially as foundations and other institutions seek to compensate for the inadequate support previously given to African Americans, women, and members of other disenfranchised groups—it is not the only end in sight. In a democratic social order, public policy and the aims of private institutions such as foundations need to be both inclusive and selective. What we do to expand opportunities for larger numbers of our citizens should not keep us from recognizing and fulfilling the justified aspirations of our most gifted few. Equity and excellence are not incompatible; we can, if we wish, make the equally great investments each requires. Neither can be achieved on the cheap, nor should one be sought at the expense of the other. A democracy has to cultivate individual excellence to ensure its own progress, the well-being of its citizens, and, possibly, its very survival.

"Separate but equal" was outlawed by the Supreme Court in *Brown* v. *Board of Education* because separate facilities and programs are inherently unequal. Not all discrimination to redress inequalities for a positive purpose has been proscribed by the courts, making it possible to maintain activities that allow opportunities of recognition both for those who are deprived and for those who are extraordinarily endowed with talent. The National Science Foundation's Minority Post-Doctoral Research Fellowship Program, for example, is offered exclusively to "underrepresented minorities" to produce especially well-trained minority and women scientists and to prepare them for positions of scientific leadership in academia. The National Institutes of Health have a similar program for researchers in the sciences. There are also private foundation-supported postdoctoral study and research opportunities for the same target population, such as the Ford Foundation's Post-Doctoral Fellowships for Minorities and the Commonwealth Fund's Fellowship Program in Academic Medicine for Minority Students.

"Reverse discrimination," as such programs are sometimes pejoratively referred to, offer opportunities—set at a high, but attainable, standard—for individual aspirants among minorities and women who may not yet be ready to compete in the parallel programs offered by the National Science Foundation and the National Institutes of Health, set at still higher standards. Of course, they are free to apply to these top programs as well. But these NSF and NIH programs benefit from those for minorities and women, which exempt them from pressure to engage in selection on bases other than merit. They are not required to give places to minority candidates at the expense of better-prepared candidates, which would lead to animosities and cynicism and deprive society of opportunities for those who are best qualified to benefit from advanced support.

Unfortunately, these carefully crafted programs for the "best" and for the best of those who deserve exceptional opportunities are challenged in the courts by insurgent, right-wing political forces. Other useful schemes have already been stopped. The court upset Pittsburgh's municipal plans for all-black public schools for boys, schools that would have presented these children with badly needed male role models. Meanwhile, a federal appeals court challenged the constitutionality of a scholarship program for black students at the University of Maryland, saying the university did not provide sufficient evidence that such scholarships are needed to correct past discrimination. As secretary of education, Lamar Alexander wanted to eliminate all compensatory programs as violations of the Civil Rights Act of 1964, and ideologues among the new Republican majority of 1994 have tried that again. Private foundations are in the vanguard supporting institutions and funding programs for minority education and professional opportunities. But when it comes to cultivating the society's human resources, foundations have other complex responsibilities. Since the 1970s, the problem is that the private foundations have felt themselves responsible for serving minority grievances, and these are not necessarily germane to identifying and supporting exceptional talent. The two issues have become confused.

The overall purpose of supporting individuals is to serve the common good. That does not mean that foundations can make a piece of the pie available to anyone and everyone who wants it. On the contrary: historically, as we will see, philanthropies have set high standards for limited programs providing scarce financial and professional support to those who are the most creative, who can define or elucidate, find solutions to or mitigate, problems. Lately, foundations have wobbled on that course in the face of pressure from charities that represent the infirm, the uneducated, the economically disadvantaged. It seems these charities believe that foundations should somehow take on the needy directly—an impossibility—rather than nurture the superior talents who, in their laboratories, might lead the society out of the morass. For example, a foundation whose historical role has been to support research on the medical frontier is now faced with pressure from groups representing victims of AIDS—who have been abandoned by government programs—to turn their support to the alleviation of the suffering of AIDS patients. Such a foundation cannot take on both roles with any effectiveness. Its role is to devote all its limited resources to research, to the laboratory.

Fair-handedness should not be the primary concern of foundation programs. The responsibility, Warren Weaver of the Rockefeller Foundation said, "is to support excellence," to consider those who are already good and help them to become better so that they may be scouts penetrating the frontiers of knowledge, opening new opportunities for the future.

In contrast to the not-for-profit world, the business world has sharply differentiated conceptions of excellence and creativity. As business craves profit, its final objective does not ordinarily include hard-to-quantify end products such as contributions to knowledge. But businessmen agree that they need highly talented individuals for their enterprises and that they do not automatically come along with MBA degrees. They have to be sought out and nurtured. Thomas Peters and Robert Waterman, Jr., concluded in their best-selling romance of big business, *In Search of Excellence,* that exceptional talents develop because numerous supports are created by businesses to encourage them, sustain them through trying times, celebrate their successes, and nurse them through failures.

The sociologist Robert Merton says the important thing is to make the right choices of individuals for the purpose. We need to "find ways of detecting potential excellence early enough to help potentiality become actuality. . . . Much human capacity for socially valued accomplishments remains latent and undeveloped." Frequently, talent "fails to find expression because it is subjected to adverse conditions." Foundations are uniquely positioned to spot talent and have total latitude for limitless searches. They are free to support individuals for any purpose and to select obvious candidates as well as to take risks on mavericks and others who have differentiated ideas. And they can encourage and fund various institutions to join them in this venture.

Talent flowers at different speeds when it is permitted to flourish at all. In the United States, we have a penchant for favoring precocity, citing special talent such as playing a musical instrument, while continuing to use exceptional IQ scores or SAT results, despite their biases and limited predictive usefulness. Colleges looking for the greatest talent now know that low SAT scores may be pegged to limited parental income, reflecting the handicaps of an impoverished life and poor schooling, handicaps that may not outlast the freshman year. According to a *New York Times* report, a Harvard alumni study over three decades found a high correlation between "success"—defined by income, community involvement, and professional satisfaction—and two freshman admission criteria: low SAT scores and a blue-collar background!

A high IQ may denote exceptional capacities of certain kinds, but those who do not score high are not necessarily less intelligent. Their intelligence, as Howard Gardner shows in *Multiple Intelligences* and other books, may take different forms. Grades are not much of an index of unusual ability either, and not at all indicative of nonacademic forms of intelligence. Individuals are rewarded for doing well on such examinations, while many who are exceptional—for example, those skilled in the arts or possessing special leadership abilities—but whose talents do not show up on tests, often struggle for recognition. Such individuals may be lost to society, as are many late bloomers. We know about their struggles to achieve status, mainly in retrospect, because of those in their ranks who eventually achieve public standing despite the odds.

Most of our society's other strategies for sorting out the best from the average are also flawed. For example, in educating our children from prekindergarten onward, we stress physical prowess and other forms of success. There are elaborate procedures for sorting out youngsters at every stage; we measure them from every possible direction. Those who do not make the grade or fail to meet expected norms face persistent discrimination. From early childhood they are given personality models to emulate. Most of these have to do with popularity. If they are not attractive all-rounders—"well liked," as Willie Loman put it in *Death of a Salesman*—they may feel like failures. To be modest, careful, reflective, noncompetitive, to be an outsider who is not "well liked" by the glamorous crowd, convinces exceptional young people that they are inferior or, even worse, idiosyncratic. Most of the two million kindergarten through high school students classified as gifted by the Federal Department of Education are bored because of the insistence on mainlining them, which keeps them from developing their exceptional capacities. In most of our schools they are hostages to the ideology of egalitarianism, discriminated against by being ignored. And nonconformism is rejected, sadly, far beyond the schoolyard. Relatively few foundations function in public schools to bring about a more sophisticated understanding of multiple intelligence among students. The Harlem Educational Activities Fund sponsored by the Daniel and Joanna S. Rose Fund is one of these, and it has found and supported exceptionally talented youngsters through tutoring, special learning opportunities, and an ongoing support net.

There is a definite need to find better ways of identifying

qualities of excellence and creative talent. No simple formulas exist for spotting talent or for giving it proper attention, and foundations will seek such formulas in vain. Simply calling individuals "creative" and their achievements "excellent" will not do. Both have become buzzwords, with so many meanings as to be little more than empty generalizations. Taking the next step of distinguishing truly exceptional individuals from the many who are simply top-notch is an extremely difficult task, because what distinguishes the highly creative person remains ill defined. It seems a task to which foundations and allied social institutions can justifiably give priority, even though it means venturing into murky waters.

Foundations have the freedom to try fresh approaches. If they grasp these opportunities, foundations will be pitted against the egalitarian and conservative tides—a uniquely American combination—that have dominated U.S. society for more than two decades. Egalitarianism and conservatism together are a powerful repressive force working against creativity. America rose to greatness as a revolutionary society following imaginative leaders. The seemingly insuperable difficulties facing U.S. society demand bursts of creative pioneering, new institutions, and new educational philosophies to provide opportunities for creative individuals to apply their talents to these problems, many of which are already nearly out of hand. Employment of those talents is indissolubly linked to both securing a civil society in which all have a stake and the dispersal of forces threatening it from the right.

Every society needs its originals, its innovators, and its educated best, who are defined not by their inheritance, connections, or wealth but rather by innate ability, education, and disciplined commitment. Tomorrow's elite will be more inclusive than the white male bastion it has been. Institutions will encompass in greater numbers the talents of women, members of ethnic minorities, and those from economically disadvantaged communities—all manner of traditional and nontraditional people with exceptional intelligence and commitment.

Private foundations are a vital part of this emergent process. Their search for our most gifted individuals and their bringing them into the foreground takes enlightened and intuitive professionals. Nurturing that talent, too, is a daunting task, as we shall discuss. "Where there is no vision, the people perish."

2

THE SUPPORT OF
INDIVIDUALS

Foundation support of individuals takes many forms: scholarships, fellowships and loans for study, and grants and awards for a great variety of specific purposes, all targeting current or future endeavors. Prizes, on the other hand, reward recent or current achievements. While the direct medium of support in grants and scholarships and fellowships and prizes is money, foundations traffic indirectly in other currencies. Their funds provide time, encouragement, the recognition of accomplishment and pathbreaking—intangible gifts all—which nurture and bolster the scientist, artist, or scholar in what are typically solitary and difficult quests.

"Grants" is an inclusive term for individual assistance, and a grant is the magic that scholars, scientists, artists, seek in order to do their work without distraction, to travel, to acquire equipment and materials. For organizations and institutions, grants permit major undertakings without the encumbering conditions set by other sources, such as private industry or governmental authorities. Of course, private foundations also set conditions for the use of their funds, but usually these conditions are more objective and can be helpful in ways government and other private and corporate capital are often not. That remains the prevailing view among applicants to private foundations. Most applicants have heard stories that wrap the grant-getting process in mystery, and rumors substitute for accurate information, especially in academia, where rumors flourish. Intelligence about foundations is a constant subject on which scientists are the best and artists the least informed. Artists are prone to believe that getting a grant depends on favoritism and that the "I like it/I don't like it" syndrome prevails. But foundation decisions in the arts are on the whole not capricious.

Awards may be given for specific projects, such as research, by underwriting the investigator in particular inquiries and/or defraying his or her living costs. A relatively rare kind of award enables individuals to work in a general field; instead of paying for a specific research project, the grant permits work in a particular discipline—such as physics or history—or across disciplines, or in a hybrid field, such as biopsychology. The focus is left to the grantee.

Other grants are given for training purposes, to enable an individual to gain greater skill in laboratory sciences, for example, or to acquire language skills. Similar grants may be given for leadership purposes, to enhance individual skills needed to play a principal role in a discipline or an institution. For example, the Rockefeller Foundation, in the darkest days of U.S.–"Red" China antagonism, enabled a handful of young scholars to learn Chinese and take other training to meet the foreseeable need for Chinese law expertise in the United States. A grant may be awarded whereby the objective is to replenish talent in an entire profession. In the 1950s, senior international legal scholars approached Dean Rusk, then president of the Rockefeller Foundation, voicing concern about the lack of talent emerging in their field. The foundation subsequently mounted a sustained effort to spot and support talent and to assist in other ways to strengthen the specialty of international legal theory.

Travel grants enable recipients who are working on a particular problem to journey from home to consult sources, confer with colleagues in their discipline, or study aspects of a current interest. Travel grants have been controversial at times because, to outsiders, they appear to be a means for entertainment or tourism, but they are not generally abused. Indeed, all kinds of individual grants may become controversial, none more than the *cause célèbre* stirred up by the well-intentioned support the president of the Ford Foundation gave to members of Robert Kennedy's principal campaign staff, all prominent Democrats, following his assassination. The idea was to afford them turn-around time. The grants fueled a congressional investigation into the way foundations fund individuals. This, in turn, led Congress to tighten the conditions that must be met in awarding such grants. As a result, some foundations—easily intimidated by vocal critics—virtually ceased making individual grants for a period of years, and in some cases altogether. In practice, the IRS administered the new regulations liberally.

There are grants to cover publication costs and/or costs associated with disseminating written, computerized, filmed, or videotaped works by individuals. Demand for these is increasing, but grants for publication and dissemination of any kind are not popular with foundations or individual donors. The usual reason given is that publication costs are an endless drain on funds, but a more important reason—rarely expressed—is that foundations shy away from endorsing the results of their grantees' research and the opinions they express. This may be shortsighted. Too many discoveries and other achievements made possible by grant funds are not well disseminated to others working in the same or related fields. Lack of publication can keep professionals and their institutions in the dark, deprived of knowledge that may be vital to their work; it can lead to duplication of effort, with a further drain on foundation funds. Presently, noteworthy dissemination efforts are being made in the literary and performing arts fields by the Lila Wallace–Reader's Digest Fund—under the heading "Audience Development" (for example, in setting up concerts for underserved rural schoolchildren)—but these efforts do not have an impact on scholarship or research. The American Council of Learned Societies receives some foundation support for dissemination of scholarship in the humanities. But the distribution of humanistic work, above all, remains seriously underfunded.

Student scholarships and loans are another form of support. They account for the majority of personal awards given by private foundations (as well as individuals). The 1994 volume of *Foundation Grants to Individuals* reports the availability of 1,270 sources of student scholarships, 225 sources of student loans, and 216 corporations offering scholarships, compared to, for example, 104 sources of research grants, 9 sources of grants for publication support.

Fellowships are ordinarily given for advanced study at colleges, universities, and research institutes. Many are for graduate students, including young professionals; others enable doctoral students to complete their dissertations or to fulfill requirements necessary for practice in their professional field; still others provide for training or retraining at advanced levels. Fellowships may also make it possible for a professional to return to formal institutional study, to catch up with or develop expertise in a particular field, or to work on a project. With today's rapid change at the frontiers of knowledge in so many disciplines and the discovery of overlap and tangents among them, there is greater need for fellowships for retraining that enables professionals to grasp the importance of achievements in allied fields. With fellowship assistance, an individual at the top of his profession may gain sufficient command and understanding of another field to facilitate his participation in interdisciplinary work or, possibly, in the creation of new fields of study.

The sciences have received generous support for the further development of investigators, and for research of all kinds, from public and private sources, as will be discussed below. With few exceptions, most of the fellowships available to artists, by contrast, are for conventional academic purposes rather than creativity on the frontiers.

There are retreats or colonies to which artists may be invited to continue with individual creative work or perhaps to collaborate with another artist. Typically, successful applicants to Yaddo, the MacDowell Colony, the Atlantic Center for the Arts, and a handful of other well-established and supported colonies are invited for six or eight weeks of complete immersion. Residents are asked to contribute to costs if they are able, whereas at the many dozens of smaller, unendowed colonies, modest per diems have to be paid. Because foundations have generally been reluctant to fund individual arts colonies, the Fund for Artists Colonies was organized to represent their common interests, with a goal of making them attractive to foundations. It was subsequently replaced by the Alliance of Artists Communities.

Akin to arts colonies are the burgeoning private-sector "think tanks" and university research institutes in the social sciences and public affairs. These offer hospitable environments for individual research and home bases for consultancy work. By now, there are more than a hundred think tanks in the United States. The Brookings Institution and the Heritage Foundation are two of the best known, the former generally considered to be liberal, the latter, distinctly conservative. For advanced scholars doing independent work, there are also study centers, such as the Center for Advanced Behavioral Studies in Palo Alto and the Institute for Advanced Study in Princeton.

A strikingly original form of residency is the master/disciple meeting in which senior scholars or practitioners join select younger professionals in the same discipline for intensive study and collegial exchanges over six to eight weeks. Master/disciple meetings play a special role in bringing along a new generation of professionals in fields that may have languished for some time. The idea also lends itself to exploring new fields or studying complex problems. The concept was pioneered by Kenneth W. Thompson, whose ideals and ideas in the social sciences, humanities, and education led to distinguished programs over several decades at the Rockefeller Foundation. International conference centers, such as the Villa Serbelloni and the Salzburg Conference Center, are ideal sites for such experiments. Some offer prolonged individual residencies for creative work.

In the 1930s, a special category of foundation support was provided for the waves of refugees from strife-torn parts of the world or for particular minority populations. The best-known effort was the placement of Jewish and other persecuted Central European intellectuals at the New School for Social Research, Bard College in one of its previous incarnations, the Institute for Advanced Study, and many universities, where they later distinguished themselves. A few foundations were similarly active in providing for Hungarian refugees in 1956. Though unrelated to contemporary foundation programs, these initiatives were forerunners of systematic efforts to assist with the special needs of women and targeted minorities.

One kind of grant foundations initiated in the past has virtually disappeared. This is the timely award by a senior foundation officer who has the authority to give unilaterally without formalities, recognizing an individual with a significant purpose or need in an openhanded and generous manner. John Gardner, when he was head of the Carnegie Corporation, would tap overworked college presidents on the shoulder and offer them a fully subsidized year off with only a few conditions, chief of which was that they were not allowed to set foot on their campuses during the year. Beneficiaries of such unsolicited generosity have said that this was the most satisfying and sometimes influential support they ever received. The common denominator was the confidence placed in them, their work, and their long-term careers. A senior natural-resources scholar who received such a grant twenty years ago "out of the blue" has recently said in tribute to then vice president Kenneth Thompson at Rockefeller, who initiated it, that he was "challenged by the confidence [Thompson] demonstrated to push as far as we could with new concepts and methods. It was much more demanding of our imagination than a project where aims and methods were specified in a funding application. This required courage and discernment on his part and I continue to salute those qualities in his actions."

Such one-to-one bets are seldom made any longer. At some foundations, officers require even the most accomplished scholars and officials to toe the same mark as rank amateurs. Perhaps this is due to burgeoning bureaucracy or fiscal conservatism or distrust of individual decisionmaking. Perhaps the fundamental problem is that foundation personnel today lack a moral reference point for recognizing exceptional individuals, exceptional artistic and scholarly ventures. Or perhaps there is a lack of sophisticated understanding of the exceptional opportunities and responsibilities foundations have as vital sources of venture capital.

There is no right way of supporting a creative person, though providing time to work is probably a common denominator for most. Available time may release the maximum potential of scholars, scientists, and artists alike. Often, there may be other impediments. Warren Weaver believed that one should discover what handicaps a scientist has and then "remove those handicaps, one at a time, in the order of their urgency."

In eighteenth-century Europe, incentives were offered to scientists in the form of prizes for achieving specific breakthroughs. The method was not successful and was superseded by conventional patronage. In the late twentieth century, prizes and the honors that go with them have made a major comeback, not as incentives but as rewards for specific results or for a series of them. The prize may of course also act as an incentive, but in truth it rarely does.

The number and variety of prizes given to Americans by governments, corporations, civic and professional associations, individuals, foundations, academic and scholarly auspices—and many others—already plentiful, is increasing. The volume *Awards, Honors and Prizes*, covering the United States and Canada, is 1,312 pages long and has 4,255 separate listings, mostly prizes. The index of sponsors is 57 pages long in telephone-book-size print; the index of awards runs to 116 pages. Instead of Sforzas of Renaissance Italy, Medicis of Florence, and kings of Spain, we have a multiplicity of donors giving medals, citations, glass bowls, copper bowls, silver bowls, gold-plated bowls, to an endless line of recipients who have earned the tribute for some deed or ongoing accomplishment. Most prizes have cash attached.

Among the more notable additions to the roster in recent years are the $150,000 awards created by the plastics millionaire H. Charles Grawemeyer. For musical composition, education, psychology, and "ideas that help improve the world order," they have the virtue not only of recognizing the individual but also of drawing attention to his or her award-winning ideas, proposals, or achievements. Similarly, the late Robert Kreidler of the Dana Foundation initiated awards honoring individuals in health and education, whose discoveries or original ideas are publicized by the foundation so that they may become known and implemented elsewhere. The new Dorothy and Lillian Gish Prize's very large award of up to $250,000 threatens to overshadow a very good idea—namely, to recognize the creativity and excellence of an artist in any art form and of any citizenship. Unlike the Oscars and

Tonys and Emmys in particular art forms, which are increasingly mired in commercialism, this award has the potential of extolling contributions to the beauty of the world. Prize-entailing film festivals, music competitions, and poetry readings are often riven with politics, success spelling an important career step for the victor.

Commercial sponsors of awards vie to exceed their competitors' antes. General Foods sponsored a prize of $200,000 after the Winrock World Food Prize raised its award to that level. The National Academy of Engineering gives an annual $350,000 prize to recognize contributions that engineering and technology make to the quality of life in the United States. In 1989, Ted Turner announced an award intended to eclipse the Nobel Prize in literature: the Turner Tomorrow Award gave $500,000 to a work of fiction and $50,000 each to four runners-up. (Turner, to no one's surprise, retained exclusive television and screen rights.) There was no encore.

The Templeton Prize for Progress in Religion was $435,000 until 1992; then Sir John Marks Templeton, in an evident move to rank with the Nobels, increased the premium to $1 million. In this world game of "Can You Top This?" Japanese electronics firms created the Praemium Imperiale—five $175,000 awards to artists. Announcing that "Japan has reached the stage where we want to make a cultural contribution to the world," the Japanese convened a quite untoppable selection committee made up of four former European prime ministers plus David Rockefeller (prime minister of a hidden U.S. government?), who enlisted Columbia's former dean of the arts, Schuyler Chapin, as his surrogate. No non-Japanese Asians were included in the prestigious jury. As could have been anticipated, these awards usually go to outstanding artists who have already been widely recognized and, one thinks, do not have a pressing need for the money.

Sponsors of the Praemium Imperiale and other lucrative awards garnered by senior establishment figures often make sen-

tentious remarks to the effect that the prize is to inspire young aspirants. Asked about this, some artists not surprisingly say this is
chicanery. What such honors and cash awards teach young composers, scientists, playwrights, etc., is that they, too, should become famous and collect great honors and vast sums.

The arts lend themselves to prizegiving. Best known in addition to those already mentioned are the Pritzker Prize in Architecture ($100,000), created in 1979; the [Leslie] Wexner Prize
($50,000) for an artist whose work "has consistently challenged
convention"; the Wolf Foundation Prizes ($100,000 divided
among scientists and artists), created by the Israeli chemist Dr. Ri-
cardo Wolf; and the Dorothy Tannen Prize ($100,000) in poetry
awarded by the Academy of American Poetry. Pulitzer Prizes
were created mostly for journalists, but drama, fiction, poetry, bi-
ography, and history are also categories. Pulitzers have gained distinction for the high standards of those who have received them,
not for the emolument, which is $3,000, although the boost to box
office and sales is often significant.

The Nobel Prizes are the most prestigious, rightly admired,
their recipients lauded and envied. What distinguishes the Nobel
Prizes in medicine, science, economics, and literature is not that
they go into six figures or that they invariably attract international
media attention but rather that they usually go to those who truly
have made original contributions that "have conferred the greatest
benefit on mankind." Only the Nobel Peace Prize has consis-
tently been controversial and sometimes reflects a remarkable lack
of imagination. In contrast, there is the Premi Internacional
Catalunya, awarded to Vaclav Havel and Richard von Weizsacker
"for the ethical dimension of their political careers" by the little-
known but highly distinguished Institut Catala d'Estudis Medi-
terranis. Four Onassis Prizes (each $250,000) are awarded in
science, culture, peace, and the environment, in the name of the
late shipping magnate.

Prizegiving in America has become an attention-getting device; honors are often given as much to celebrate the donor as the recipient. The first MacArthur Prize Fellowships may be partially responsible, because of the front-page attention they unexpectedly received. What some have learned from the MacArthur experience is that there can be a mutual payoff: winners receive dollars and recognition, presenters get publicity and prestige. (Celebrity may be the most prize recipients eventually achieve.) There is some evidence to show that recipients of major prizes, such as the Nobel, do not make significant contributions thereafter. There are exceptions, but the proposition deserves further investigation.

Winners and donors of prizes become public figures because of strong media interest. But there is another explanation for the coverage: ordinarily, the press and other media are not interested in what foundations do, or in the not-for-profit culture in general; the press responds to prizes because the public likes heroes—and the sudden convergence of money and fame constitutes the heroic in our culture. We create heroes (and goats) all the time. The media's interest is in prizewinners per se, in their personalities, their personal lives, their newfound wealth. The work for which they received the award is often given cursory coverage. Certainly, little attention is paid to the work if it requires more than an easy explanation and simple understanding. The country's favorite recipients are those already well known, such as Kennedy Center honorees.

In 1978, the first year those awards were conferred, the honorees were Fred Astaire, Marian Anderson, Richard Rodgers, Arthur Rubinstein, and George Balanchine, all "artists who have made significant contributions to American culture through their careers in the performing arts." The purpose ostensibly remained the same (in addition to raising money for the Kennedy Center), but by the mid-1980s, the awards had deteriorated, the annual ceremony distorted to suit a different caste: Perry Como, Irene Dunne, Pete Seeger, Kirk Douglas, Roy Acuff, etc.

The National Medal of Arts was intended to be an even more significant award for "outstanding contributions to the excellence, growth, support, and availability of the arts in the United States." Ralph Ellison, Agnes de Mille, Saul Bellow, Leontyne Price, and Alfred Eisenstadt are distinguished recipients of the medal. Pressure to bring even the nation's highest arts award down to a common denominator level led to subsequent presentation of the medal to Minnie Pearl, José Ferrer, Pete Seeger (again), Roy Acuff (again), etc.

Americans have a romance with titles, with success, more than with achievement; with personalities, not with superior artistry. Thus prizegiving is often more gamesmanship than the serious reward of noteworthy achievements. It is more competition among individuals and institutions seeking public attention than spotlighting the achievements of exceptionally creative people.

Is the public attention big prizes generate good for the arts as a whole or for medical research or historical scholarship? Answers conflict; distinguished awards given by a rigorous selection process employing impeccable scholars or scientists or artists do ennoble their professions as well as the recipients. Other prizes have a dubious impact. Prize recipients are democratized by becoming popularized: they are not different, they do not stand out for excelling at something. We make them our heroes by making them one of us.

Opportunities for independent work are especially vital to the lives of artists and humanists. But Americans today appear to understand that less—and perhaps value artists' and humanists' contributions to society less—than past generations. John Adams, among others of our intellectual Founding Fathers, keenly appreciated the place of the artist in society. "I must study Politics and War that my sons may have the liberty to study Mathematics and Philosophy," Adams wrote in 1780. "My sons ought to study Mathematics and Philosophy, Geography, Natural History [etc.]

in order to give their Children a right to study Painting, Poetry, Musick, Architecture, Statuary, Tapestry and Porcelaine."

What has happened to that vision? In the 1990s as in previous decades, private American philanthropy contributed most to religious and educational organizations, least to the arts and humanities. *Giving USA 1995* reports that "art, culture and humanists received $9.7 billion from all sources in 1994. This compares with $58.9 billion received by religious organizations the same year."

How are artists faring—especially creative, originating artists—in public and private foundation programs?

Like other productive members of society and more than most, artists need financial support and other encouragement. The best of them are continuously innovative, daring, and willing experimenters who, like scientists, accept failure as part of progress. They persist in their quest without certainty of success. They need help to do their work, and recognition even more.

"In a vital community," Herbert Read wrote in *The Politics of the Unpolitical*, "art is promoted in three ways: socially by appreciation, economically by patronage and essentially by liberty." Artists depend upon appreciation, patronage, and freedom to create. Some great artists have worked without immediate appreciation: Van Gogh, for example. But such individuals are rare. Artists largely support themselves. They are chief subsidizers of the muses through their unpaid or underpaid labors. Working spouses or mates are the second most important source of an artist's livelihood. Historically, artists' hardships have been rationalized: "Artists must struggle and suffer" has long been invoked to excuse the living conditions that many artists are forced to endure. Cyril Connolly called this ideology of deprivation "fatuous romantic fatalism . . . 'if it's in you, it's bound to come out' is a wish-fulfillment. More often, it stays in and goes bad."

Today, traditional patronage from public and private sources is not a major factor in the work of a high percentage of American artists. They receive less direct support from foundations now than in the 1950s and 1960s. According to a survey commissioned privately, by the early 1980s fewer than 10 percent of foundations that give to the arts provide direct grants to support artists. The sociologist Paul J. DiMaggio points out that "despite the apparent autonomy of the private foundation and diversity of the foundation universe, most foundation arts dollars go quietly to major established institutions."

A National Endowment for the Arts planning document categorized the relative attractiveness of arts institutions or areas to private funding, while underscoring the unattractiveness of support of individuals in the private sector:

Attractive to Private Sector	Less Attractive to Private Sector	Unattractive to Private Sector
Major museum exhibitions	Classical theater	Avant-garde and interdisciplinary
Opera	Modern dance	*Support of individuals*
Ballet	Jazz	
Orchestras	Design	Visual artists organizations
Large presenters and performing arts centers	Film preservation	Postmodern dance
	Folk arts	Video preservation
	Public radio	Museum maintenance
Institutions undertaking capital construction	New music	
	Media arts centers	Minority organizations
	Chamber music	
	Arts education	Archives and libraries
Public television	Choral music	
Arts presentations	Professional training	Service organizations
	Museum conservation	
	Medium and small presenters	Dance notation
	Artist colonies	

What remains of individual artists' support at most of the largest foundations is driven by those foundations' social and political agendas—a reflection of self-directed, narcissistic behavior. Politically correct grantmaking, much of it multicultural, predominates.

Given that some foundations in the past have been less responsive to the work of minority and women artists, it is understandable that they are now applying great pressure to redress or remedy that neglect and to support programs focused on those groups. The $5–$7 million yearly arts budget at the Ford Foundation today is devoted to multicultural and intercultural projects and to minority artists and institutions. These are the foundation's priorities; quality per se has become a secondary consideration, a situation both lamentable and destructive. Anytime that quality is not the primary focus—without regard for race and gender—our culture is diminished, just as it was undoubtedly diminished by the blindness of foundations in the past to talent when it sprang up in women or in ethnic contexts.

"Quality is now considered a code word for racism or elitism in most philanthropic circles," Robert Brustein has pointed out. At many foundations, programs are so narrowly and insistently focused on "cultural diversity" and "multiculturalism" that "the entire cultural world," in Brustein's description, is "bending itself into contortions in order to find the right shape for grants under the new criteria." Brustein aptly calls this "coercive philanthropy." He does not exaggerate. His is prominent among those few who will not cut their artistic jib to fit the foundation's sail. Ford Foundation president Franklin A. Thomas's rebuttal to this assertion has been lame and virtually confirms Brustein's assertion. Ford, Thomas replied, supports "collaborations between artists in the United States and their counterparts in Africa, Asia and Latin America"; and Ford has programs to "strengthen financial stability" and "the civic role" of artists and to "preserve cultural traditions." Not a word about artistic vision or quality.

The Ford Foundation's distinguished cultural program under W. McNeil Lowry in the 1960s and 1970s has been narrowed in scope and scale and is now devoted primarily to the support of minority artists and minority arts institutions. Rockefeller, MacArthur, and Wallace also have multicultural agendas in the arts. They may be misjudging and possibly even demeaning the interests of creative minority artists and of minority audiences. What is certain is that these foundations have forgone an earlier vision and priority of excellence.

The MacArthur Foundation's cultural program is focused on Chicago and Florida, where the MacArthur family lived and their businesses were located. The Pew Trust has a modest individual support program, created and directed until 1994 by Ella King Torrey, which is confined to the Philadelphia region. The Rockefeller Foundation, noted in previous decades for innovative arts programs and direct support of originating artists, now supports artists overwhelmingly only if they "advance international and inter-cultural understanding." The Lila Wallace–Reader's Digest Fund maintains a small program for writers out of its huge $45 million arts budget. In 1993, this budget mostly went to increasing audiences, encouraging minorities, expanding marketing by arts institutions, and to libraries and literacy. Mellon, too, makes grants to strengthen the administration of arts institutions but does not give direct support to artists. Only small to medium-sized foundations, such as Bush, Whiting, Lannan, McKnight, and Guggenheim, focus on the needs of originating artists. Apart from such efforts, there remains the grantmaking by state and regional arts councils and the National Endowment for the Arts.

Individual grant giving by public sources has always been under fire and subject to intense political infighting in its decision-making. Because applications to the NEA are unlimited, anyone may apply in each artistic category, regardless of ability, experience, or talent. This creates a huge, undifferentiated applicant load. Appointments to selection committees are politically sensitive, given the NEA's need to serve constituencies everywhere, but especially those of key members of Congress.

The NEA made grants to composers and choreographers in its first year, 1965, but by 1968, the House voted to prohibit the Endowment from making grants to individuals. The prohibition did not last, but the issue has hung in the balance ever since, sometimes provoking intraoffice battles that rival the attacks by censorious senators and representatives. Championing direct support of artists in the program mix, Nancy Hanks, who was NEA chair from 1969 to 1977, had a hard time with friends as well as foes. Representative Paul Engle, a powerful supporter from Iowa, fumed that expenditures for costumes for *Aïda* at the Metropolitan Opera "would have supported all the poets in America for a year." Senator Claiborne Pell, an NEA supporter, complained that forty-eight grants were made in a year to abstractionists and only twelve to representational artists. But the principal danger to the Endowment as a whole has come from grassroots attacks and especially now from the religious right attacking works that it finds offensive or that seem frivolous or just incomprehensible to vocal citizens and their representatives. The Christian Coalition, in alliance with Speaker Gingrich, Majority Leader Dick Armey, and other leading Republicans in the House and Senate, want to scuttle the NEA and the National Endowment for the Humanities. During the summer of 1995, they came close to building the coalition needed to prevent reauthorization of the Endowments. They succeeded in decimating the staff of the Endowments and in forcing the NEA to reorganize into four program areas. Support of individual artists was virtually eliminated.

Jane Alexander, the current NEA chair, has the unenviable task of balancing support of free artistic inquiry and cutting-edge performance while maintaining a viable Endowment. In 1994, she eliminated regranting—the process by which an NEA-supported institution could use its funds to support individual artists. Ms. Alexander knows that only the NEA's education activities and those offering arts access to the "underserved" are politically viable. And there is another source of pressure on NEA funding of creative artists. The manifold increase in arts "support" organizations hungry for larger shares of the NEA budget pie heightens competition for available funds and has eroded support by NEA staff members for direct individual support activities. This growth in arts bureaucracies and their appetites is becoming as much of a problem in the arts as it is in public education and will have to be dealt with on a policy level. Right now foundations subvent more arts support organizations than artists who do the work.

The support of Congress and the public for science students, investigators, and researchers stands in marked contrast to the penuriousness of the support offered to artists (and humanists, as we will see later) at all levels. Both the National Science Foundation and the National Institutes of Health offer training, study, and research grants in fields of science and engineering, many of them for five years at $35,000 to $50,000 and more per year, plus annual supplements of at least $10,000 for materials and travel costs. Scientists with these awards are free to take risks, to do whatever they wish. There are separate programs at NIH and NSF specifically for "underrepresented minorities," to encourage their entry and career development in biomedical and behavioral research and teaching. These parallel programs serve training and development purposes while also shielding the principal support programs from political agendas that might otherwise impact standards of selection. There are a few comparable programs in the sciences in the private sector, at such corporations as Bell Labs, and at foundations, most notably that at the Alfred P. Sloan Foundation. Artists and humanists lack the same richness of opportunities through the NEA and NEH and in the private sector.

Humanists have the least abundant resources. Except for the

Guggenheim Foundation's program supporting humanities scholars, the Whiting Foundation's thesis-year fellowships, and the
Andrew W. Mellon Foundation's generous support of graduate
fellowships, libraries, and other humanistic institutions, private
foundation support of the humanities has been terribly neglected.
In early 1995, the secretary of the Mellon Foundation estimated
that the humanities receive *less than 1 percent* of all foundation
support, totaling approximately $44 million from the 832 largest
foundations and less than $6 million from the rest. The additional
10 to 13 percent of foundation "cultural" funding is mostly swal-
lowed up by libraries, museums, and major arts institutions, by
the alarming increase in costly arts support organizations, and by
grants for marketing and other logistical work performed by a
new breed of arts bureaucrats. The NEH's $150 million in grants
annually in support of scholarly study of American history and
culture represent two-thirds of all grants awarded in the humanities by public and private foundations combined.

Is the discrepancy between our investments in scientists and
artists a true measure of our nation's value system? Or is the discrepancy the consequence of ignorance about how artists and humanists work and what they need in order to do so?

Artists and humanists do not get the same research and development opportunities as scientists, yet they need both. They, too,
must maintain a spirit of pure inquiry and curiosity about our culture; they provide an alternative perspective on society to the one
of material wealth by which we primarily measure ourselves.
They present images of different value systems, ideas, and ways of
living; they critique, challenge, and clarify existing paradigms of
the culture and, as the sculptor Leonard Hunter has pointed out,
reflect "the internal landscape of dreams, spiritual experiences and
self-awareness" of all of us.

Artists and scientists work much the same way toward similar
ends. "Failure"—the litmus paper turning blue rather than red—is

endemic to the work and success of both. The creative artist posits a purpose and may work for years to discover the right solution, if ever. Art and science are complementary, providing different aspects of human experience; both contribute in their own ways to a deeper awareness of ourselves. Indeed, most of the important scientific discoveries of this century demand extraordinary imagination and clarity of values to avoid their abuse or disastrous misuse. Thus the scientist needs the artist and the humanist.

Humanists and artists record our heritage and communicate our cultural values; they also enable us better to imagine the world we are creating through scientific discovery and technological changes and help us to take responsibility for our actions.

The only alternative, if the Endowments cannot supply adequate means, is that the private foundations be persuaded to give priority to research and innovation, and to the material needs and encouragement of our artists and humanists, who—like scientists, engineers, technologists—work on society's frontiers. But asked in the summer of 1995 if they expect to replace the Endowments' dollars if they are eliminated or sharply cut, foundation officers and board members across the country were unanimous in saying that while they are sympathetic to the purposes involved, their institutions' policies and program commitments leave no available funds to deal with any of the new demands on them that are a result of congressional actions dropping or seriously reducing support of human services, education, and, prospectively, the arts and humanities. Their reactions reveal great sensitivity in guarding the independence and individuality of their institutions against the fallout from the exigencies of governmental actions. They are quietly determined to defend their autonomy. M. Christine DeVita, president of the DeWitt Wallace– and Lila Wallace–Reader's Digest Funds, has said: "The mission of the Lila Wallace–Reader's Digest Fund is clear and we are committed to it. Our grantmaking is driven by our mission to build audiences for the arts. Just as our grantmaking focus is limited, so are our resources—we don't have extra funds to give out." And Harold M. Williams, president of the J. Paul Getty Trust, testifying in Washington in favor of maintaining viable arts and humanities agencies, asserted: "I can state with absolute confidence that private funding, which is already inadequate to meet the legitimate need of our arts and cultural institutions, certainly could not substitute for the Endowments were the latter not reauthorized."

3

MACARTHUR'S LONG-TERM SUPPORT

A prize or a year's project grant offers encouragement to individuals because they have been singled out for support, but in some instances this is not enough. Creative persons need *long-term* support to develop and to do significant work; this is the great enhancement of a multiyear grant. The National Institutes of Health recognized this in creating the lifetime career research awards in science and engineering and ten-year awards for young investigators in biomedical sciences (both were replaced by programs of shorter duration in recent years). In the private sector especially, the Rockefeller Foundation and, later, the Sloan Fund, Pew, and a few others have also supported science and medical researchers for more than a year at a time.

Social scientists, artists, and humanists have mostly lacked opportunities for sustained support; most of their grants are for a year or less. For artists especially, this has been a drawback because their creativity has a rhythm that is burdened and threatened either by no support at all or by the shameful annual frenzy of soliciting grants. The work of creative individuals is seriously interrupted and may be jeopardized by a frequent need to complete new applications for vital financial support. The problem is further exacerbated if the applicant also has to create a new project annually rather than simply admit, "I want to continue painting" or "I want to continue working on my book." At the same time, many applicants feel obliged to report grandiose results for the previous year. The entire machinery then has to be cranked up again twelve months later.

Multiyear awards have a greater potential. Prolonged security allows humanists, artists, and social scientists (like scientists) to take risks that may lead to creative accomplishments beyond anything likely to be attained with short-term support. When chosen carefully, selected artists, scholars, and scientists who are given sustained support can achieve something that would not otherwise be possible. This fact underlies the "value-added" concept, a much-spoken mantra in the foundation world. The implication of the value-added grant is that it may help to shape and direct the recipient's career in a significant way. In a larger context, it may place the individual in a position to make an exceptional contribution to the world. The premise is that cultivating a textured vision, for example, takes lucid concentration that is made possible only by gainful *artistic* employment. With guaranteed multiyear support, creative work can truly be undertaken full time. For women artists, that has the additional advantage of reconciling care for children with assured artistic or scholarly productivity over time.

The most innovative current program of this kind is the Mac-Arthur Foundation Fellowships, originally called the Prize Fellowships. In its first fifteen years, more than 450 fellows have been named, with awards from $150,000 to $375,000 over five years—$30,000 to $75,000 annually—depending on the age of the recipient, plus full health insurance. These most coveted individual awards not only are long term but also are given to individuals to use as they see fit; they are not tied to a project or a specific purpose. They can be used to develop a talent, to pursue current interests or one or more creative tasks. The recipients can set their sights on ambitious goals or new approaches to their subject or medium; they can stretch the boundaries of a discipline, learn new techniques, or perhaps work collaboratively with others.

Assured assistance over time cultivates resourcefulness and patience; financial independence builds up an artist's resistance to the temptations of what is commercially profitable at the expense of an artistic vision. Long-term support encourages young researchers to develop their talents fully, allows those in midcareer to persist in their view or to navigate a midlife change of focus, and frees senior scholars, scientists, and artists to make synthesizing statements. Regardless of career stage, it bestows the rare, yet vital, freedom to fail and start over. Among potential recipients in all professions, such awards possess a very special status. Getting one of them is like winning the jackpot on a quiz show or holding the winning ticket in a lottery. That is how rare they are.

There is a qualitative distinction between awards that are tenable over two or three years and those, like the MacArthur fellowships, that offer five or more years. It is not simply a matter of more money over more time. Most creative people can visualize at the outset what they can do in two or three years; five years is a different proposition altogether. Such support opens up questions as to whether or not to make career changes or to take on an open-ended project that was deferred for lack of time and other resources. Said one playwright upon receiving a five-year fellowship: "Three years is a generous grant; five years is a life."

These long-term unrestricted opportunities offered by the MacArthur Foundation's fellowships were the result of fortuitous circumstances and the determination of an unusual group of individuals. The story of the creation of the MacArthur Foundation is well known, but what is less well known are the meetings, decisions, and strategizing before the first Prize Fellowships were given—a kind of paradigm for both the triumphs and the pitfalls of grantmaking, which we are concerned with here. In spring 1979, some scholars and leading professionals were brought together at the Century Association in Manhattan to consider "a possible program for individual awards," which, they were told, was to be different from anything that had preceded it in the private sector. The awards were to be long term and, as it turned out, would leave it to recipients to decide how to spend the generous funds they received. What finally emerged was the result of a twelve-month consultation process, which was well under way when the two days of Century meetings took place.

The John D. and Catherine T. MacArthur Foundation hosted the meeting. Two of its board members, Roderick MacArthur, son of the founder, and William Kirby, the founder's lawyer, introduced the concept of the new program. They had become interested upon receiving a letter from Dr. George Burch, a dean at Tulane University, who had written to the newly created foundation that it was a shame for scientists doing important work to have to interrupt their progress with annual grant applications. "Impressing review committees and dealing with pressure to publish [are] a waste of time," Burch wrote. He proposed a private program of long-term support of scientists by MacArthur comparable to NIH and NSF public programs. Rod MacArthur sanctified the idea by asserting somewhat extravagantly that his late father would approve of a program to discover and support geniuses like Einstein. From the beginning, the idea was expanded to include especially creative people in other fields as well.

To lead the research process, the foundation hired F. Champion Ward, who had retired as vice president of the Ford Foundation, and, on Ward's recommendation, myself, then a dean at New York City's Hunter College, and before that a Rockefeller Foundation officer with experience running individual grant programs. Working with a committee of the board, we considered all facets of the program, soliciting advice from professionals in many fields. Inquiries were supplemented by exhaustive research about other programs, such as those at the Alfred P. Sloan Foundation, the Institute of Current World Affairs, the John Simon Guggenheim Memorial Fund, the Rockefeller Foundation, and university-based programs such as Harvard's Junior Fellowships. The board's committee held monthly meetings, usually in Chicago. These included Kirby; Acting MacArthur President John Corbally, formerly president of the University of Illinois; Jerome Wiesner, then recently retired as president of MIT; Edward Levi, former U.S. Attorney General and former president of the University of Chicago; and Robert D. Ewing, president of Bankers Life, the holding corporation for the MacArthur billions. The chairman was Rod MacArthur, who, with great determination and endless manipulation, made this "his" program from the start. Without his perseverance, a program might not have emerged.

Gathered around a table at the Century on April 23 and 24, 1979, was a stellar cast, including Jerome Wiesner, Edward Levi, Saul Bellow, Nobel laureate in literature, cultural historian Charles Frankel, sociologist Robert Merton, geographer Gilbert White, Dr. Jonas Salk, recognized around the world for creating a polio vaccine, physicist John Wheeler, biologist Robert Morison, *New York Times* architecture critic Ada Louise Huxtable, and Professor McGeorge Bundy of NYU, who was formerly a national security adviser and the president of the Ford Foundation. Near the discussion's outset, Bundy remarked that one of the most important things U.S. society can do is give unrestricted encouragement over significant periods of time to individuals of unusual promise. Instead, he pointed out, the society's inertial forces tend to constrain the efforts of such persons. Bundy underscored giving opportunities to exceptionally talented individuals for what they most want to do, defined by themselves, not by external forces.

Most of those in the room agreed with Bundy. Both days' discussions focused on whom to single out, who should do the looking, what other specific purposes an exceptional award of the kind being contemplated might have. All the participants were bent on influencing the MacArthur trustees as to how to spend their vast millions. Jonas Salk recalled how, when he was forty years of age, Allen Gregg, Warren Weaver's successor at the Rockefeller Foundation, advised him to choose to do "that which makes your heart leap." Basil O'Connor, of the National Foundation of the March of Dimes, also afforded a turning point for Salk, by creating an opportunity for him to do work outside of normal laboratory patterns. Salk advised MacArthur to create a program that would enable people to train in a discipline other than one they were in and also to create an ambience that would encourage people to change fields. He and others around the table held that it was important to find the right "choosers" of talent but equally essential for the foundation later to care for its grantees as Gregg and O'Connor had cared for Salk. This theme, the importance of ongoing supportiveness, came up again and again. Ada Louise Huxtable and Fred Friendly, previously with CBS, now at Columbia University, emphasized addressing "thoughtful and creative people in society" and not giving the awards to mediocre talent. Others, too, were concerned not to waste the opportunity and suggested giving priority to people who had already had a distinguished career and wished to make a capstone contribution. Some speakers made a special case for people in particular professions.

"How do you provide against orthodoxy?" Champ Ward interjected, raising the issue of how the program could embrace the unusual person. His question set off a discussion of the value of "mavericks," also referred to less kindly by some as "queer ducks" or "odd ducks." No subject received more attention on both days than defining the kinds of persons the new program should be for and how they should be treated. Individuals at the table had different ideas as to why recipients should be chosen: for their specific interests, to enable them to change fields, to gain new expertise, to leave a profession in order to do something they want to do very badly. Some said preference should be given to people "who are going to help us see things differently"; others emphasized those who would come up with unifying ideas and concepts; still others advocated those likely to create the disciplines of the future, people who would explore independently. They proposed singling out individuals who wanted to make a difference, unconventional explorers, atypical people, mavericks, inconspicuous people who would make the vital difference in creating community and social change, people with synergistic power, people who catalyze.

The rest of the first day's discussions centered on the role of talent scouts, selectors, and trustees in deciding on award recipients. Two variations of a system were favored. Robert Morison explained the long successful fellowship process at the Rockefeller Foundation, in which scouts in the field proposed fellows, who were more or less approved routinely by the New York office. The other idea, preferred by some, was to give a decisionmaking role to a selection committee that would receive nominations from scouts. Staff work would be important in making either system work.

The second day's discussion focused on the characteristics desired of candidates and of the seekers of the talented—the scouts and nominators. Describing the venture at that moment as more than an idea and less than a program, Champ Ward asked those assembled to concentrate on how to identify nominees and select awardees.

Charles Frankel said these "majestic awards" were most needed by imaginative professionals who should not be narrow academics. American high culture, he said, was in the process of degenerating into essentially hyperspecialized monastic fields. Others who spoke shared the view that candidates should be sought among interdisciplinary university scholars. They disagreed with those who said greater priority should be given to high-risk people who would produce the greatest payoff, extraordinarily gifted individuals who should not be bound to a subject or project. Robert Fuller, a physicist who had been president of Oberlin College, suggested putting money on people who have not already proved themselves. What about people outside the university, Fuller asked rhetorically, people who are doing things that will change the world in ways that are not visible? Fuller also cited the Princeton literary critic R. P. Blackmur, to whom Fuller had talked shortly before his death. Evaluating his life, Blackmur said he did not prize his own books and articles as much as his "incubation" of numerous other people, whom he had enabled to grow. Fuller went on to observe that there could be tremendous leverage gained if the new program could identify those people who can perform that function in society, then free them to do it. A great teacher and a great foundation administrator are exemplars. Their product will be invisible and disappear into society, but it will support and make possible ten times more creativity than if they had chosen to write their own book. In the renewed discussions of mavericks that ensued, Jerome Wiesner remarked that the most creative people are not always the soundest in their field. The procedure for identifying candidates would face the tricky task of getting the right balance of imagination, irresponsibility, and soundness. Some of these were issues at the nub of the program when the MacArthur Prize Fellows Program was implemented later that year; some were not fully resolved and remain challenging issues for those who today administer individual grant programs.

The group agreed that, among those to be considered, the youthful explorers would be difficult to select compared to those who want to change course in midcareer or those reaching some terminal point in their career who wish to pick up a new issue or idea to work on. The midcareer gamble, said Wiesner, is better than the early gamble, where one is identifying people on the basis of much less data. The majority agreed that young people prosper if they are in a strong intellectual environment, if they have some challenge from older peers. Saul Bellow said literary life had been dried out by the universities; young artists needed some other kind of center to be part of to keep them from circulating around in "a sort of canine nervousness."

As they got down to the specifics of identifying candidates, the group focused on the characteristics of the choosers. Said Charles Frankel, one needs people of taste and sensitivity who do not pay attention to peer review but rather go for talent. Robert Merton put forward the concept of the scout as a "human equivalent of the truffle hound." Judges of quality, including those who are themselves mavericks, are to be found in every field and could act as sources of talent at every age and expertise level. Merton's proposal led to the general conclusion that candidates should be identified by qualified individuals specially recruited for the purpose.

Gilbert White and the Canadian political scientist Crawford Goodwin proposed a mix of scouts made up of designated experts and foundation staff. The latter they hoped would be "Henry Moe types," referring to the distinguished long-term head of the John Simon Guggenheim Memorial Foundation, who had a brilliant record of spotting talent.

Before adjourning, the group discussed an innovation tried only a few times before: Final selection should be absolute, not competitive. The foundation would seek an absolute standard of quality in its prize fellows; the search and the awards should be unlimited and proceed year round. The experts were unanimous that the MacArthur trustees should not get involved in the selection process; they should approve the fellows recommended to them. Roderick MacArthur and William Kirby listened politely.

4

TRUSTEES: ALMONERS AND RISK TAKERS

The MacArthur trustees approved the Prize Fellows Program in September 1979, and remaining procedural questions were settled by February of the following year, when I was appointed program director. In July 1980, the first of one hundred nominators were invited to propose candidates, and less than a year later, the selection committee, having considered two hundred candidates, forwarded twenty-one names to the full MacArthur board.

The recommendations provoked a memorable battle. The twenty-one included six scientists, four social scientists, a social activist, and six writers. Some board members, assuming that the Prize Fellowships would go mostly to scientists, had not expected so many writers or other artists and humanists to be recommended. One board member, the president of a large bank in Chicago, confided to the group that he himself wrote poetry before breakfast every morning; why, he asked, did poets need money to write? He and others questioned the proposed awards to Robert Penn Warren and to Derek Walcott and Joseph Brodsky, who in later years were to win Nobel Prizes in literature. Several other names on the list of twenty-one were questioned as well. Board members disputed the selection committee's recommendations (even though several board members sat on the committee) as if the staff work and committee deliberations over a year counted for nothing. For a time it was touch-and-go whether a majority of the board would accept or reject half the candidates.

Edward Levi turned the tide. Despite his reluctance to get involved in controversy, Levi spoke on behalf of the humanists and their mission. Recalcitrant board members retreated in the face of their conservative colleague's defense of writers and, on sober reflection, worried about the adverse publicity should selection committee members resign if their recommendations were rejected.

Overwhelmingly favorable media reaction to the first group of Prize Fellows mollified most of the skeptical trustees, but the fact that the board had questioned the judgments of a selection committee of very distinguished members the board itself had appointed had a chilling effect on members of the committee. Ten of the twenty it recommended for fellowships six months later were scientists. Sitting next to me at a board luncheon around this time, board member William Simon—the business tycoon and former secretary of the Treasury—turned and said, "That's a horse's-ass program you're running, don't you agree?" Perhaps because of this irascibility, Simon, unlike other board members, stood up to Roderick MacArthur and ultimately resigned from the board rather than knuckle under to him in later disputes.

The MacArthur trustees may have been a particularly volatile group—with accusations, threats, lawsuits, and counteraccusations breaking out into the open—but Rod MacArthur was the chief protagonist of the strife. Personal acrimony among MacArthur trustees was not unusual in the foundation's early years. It was not until MacArthur's death in 1984 and the replacement of President Corbally, until Elizabeth McCormack became chair and Margaret Mahoney joined her on the board, that civil relationships and proper procedures could be established.

Most foundation boards are sedate by comparison and do not let even their most serious disagreements get into the media. Foundation boards are structured like corporate boards. Large independent foundations have boards of fifteen to twenty-five members who meet monthly or quarterly, with executive and other committees meeting in between. Most family foundations hold a single "annual" meeting or at most quarterly ones. Their ongoing business may be run by a lawyer or banker or a senior family member.

The composition and role of today's foundation boards are evolving, some obviously, others more subtly. Traditionally, foundation trustees have had a unique role. Both public servants and private almoners, they have guarded the public trust of a private philanthropy. Trustees of major foundations in the past were prominent figures drawn from public life (government service), the professions (especially law), and universities (presidents), and were successful old-line businessmen—all members of establishments who regarded themselves as stewards husbanding major fortunes, carrying out explicit or general instructions of a foundation's benefactor. In addition to their fiduciary responsibilities, trustees today hire (and may fire) the foundation's CEO (if the foundation has a staff). They decide strategic directions and specific objectives (in consultation with a staff), creating a budget to carry them out and oversee expenditures. They are supposed to understand the mission of the foundation.

Trustees of major independent foundations have recognized that they cannot fulfill their obligations without the services of professional staff. Most of the largest independent foundations have a paid staff that reviews and investigates proposals (if their institutions accept them), develops projects, and interacts with the public. In 1992, the W. K. Kellogg Foundation reported staff in all categories numbering 229, Rockefeller 142, Ford 590. But there are many other large foundations—the Brown Foundation of Houston, for example, with assets of about $600 million—that are poorly staffed (in the 1980s, Brown had one full-time person). Community foundations, on the other hand, have the highest percentage of paid staff. Corporate foundations' staffs are often administrators who became sidetracked from major avenues of corporate power. In recent years, corporate foundation staff have suffered sharp reductions, apparently victims of downsizing. Of the foundations surveyed by the Foundation Center in 1993, only one out of four reported paid staff; those with assets less than $5 million, only one out of eight. Few if any of the 26,000 smaller foundations, not included in the survey, have any paid staff. What passes for staff reported by many medium and small foundations are often secretarial and clerical people. Thus trustees at the vast majority of foundations take on staff functions of all kinds as well as ultimate decisionmaking responsibility.

Historically, the lawyers, bankers, government servants, successful businessmen, and university presidents who dominated foundation boards—especially the large independent foundations and the growing number of community foundations—were well suited to their responsibilities. Fiscal conservatives, they husbanded the assets through prudent investments for which their privileged positions gave them up-to-date knowledge. Significantly, conservatism extended to understanding the limits of their role in carrying out the programs of the foundation. Those, they realized, were the business of the president and staff. The trustees' role as they saw it was to create overall policy and to support the staff as long as its leadership enjoyed the trustees' confidence. This meant that initiatives of great significance for a field could be undertaken with staff assurance that the risks involved would not jeopardize their jobs. There was, for example, the inquiry into the country's patterns of sexual behavior that led to the unprecedented, controversial Kinsey Reports of 1948 and 1953, which would not have been possible without a series of Rockefeller Foundation grants. The subject was a delicate one for most of Rockefeller's very proper trustees. They nevertheless backed the president and staff because of the importance of the project, although it was sure to embroil the foundation in controversy (it did). By contrast, when private foundations were needed to support the survey *Sexual Practices in the United States,* conducted in 1992 and published in 1994—the Bush administration had caved in to conservative pressure and withdrawn the project's government financing—no foundation was prepared to take on the project. Finally, a group of foundations banded together and put up a much-reduced budget that undercut some of the survey's findings. Another example from the past: A traditional board of trustees without an artist member was asked in the early 1960s by its staff to allocate one million dollars to create the Columbia-Princeton Electronic Music Studio. They listened painfully and incredulously to a sample of such music. When the staff, under questioning, assured them that electronic music was a significant development in musical composition, the trustees unhesitatingly and unanimously voted in support of the proposal. During the same period—the 1950s and 1960s—trustees at Ford and Rockefeller, working closely with their staffs, took the initiative in shifting major program funds to the training of academic and public leadership in developing countries of Asia, Africa, and Latin America. Again in this instance, trustees exercised leadership in progressive and often risky policies and programs. They acted courageously and decisively.

The boards of the past were far from perfect. They were overwhelmingly male and white. Most of them were slow to sympathize with the plight of minorities and with the struggle of women for equal standing, slow to overcome anti-Semitic prejudices.

Many of those elected to foundation boards in that era were, as in some places today, members of interconnected premier families. They believed themselves natural choices for nonprofit-foundation trustee roles and were groomed for them by family teaching and lore at the schools they attended, through the traditions and habits of their social circles.

Foundation trustee responsibilities today have become too complex to be prepared for around the family dinner table. But to appreciate today's changing needs, it is not necessary to belittle the success of the traditional and, by and large, conservative foundation boards of the past. Indeed, one cannot help but respect the way they carried out their responsibilities.

Trustees today are confronted with a wide range of governance problems. The propensity of wealthy benefactors to appoint their offspring and other family members or cronies as trustees is a chronic problem that bedevils family foundations and weakens the effectiveness of other board members. Philanthropies are not well served if they become the hobbyhorse of surviving relatives who are ill equipped by lack of education, experience, ability, or interest to direct them. They can do harm by just taking up valuable board slots and being inattentive or absent. In this way, the assets of many small to medium-sized foundations are left to be managed de facto by the family lawyer or are inherited by bank trustees or become homogenized in a community trust. In other instances, family members assert themselves as more equal than the other trustees, which is what happened in the early years of the MacArthur Foundation. Other trustees may pander to family members as if to a royal succession. Whatever its origin, entrenched board leadership whose primary interest is self-interest rather than the purposes of the foundation is always undesirable. It subverts the foundation.

The conservative broker, banker, or business executive trustee of the past often understood that not-for-profit enterprises had distinct purposes and a different ethic than profitmaking ones, and treated them accordingly. J. Irwin Miller is often cited as the ideal businessman in philanthropy. For many years head of his own exemplary Cummins Engine Foundation, he served on the Ford Foundation, Yale University, and a host of other major boards. He immersed himself creatively and sensitively in their possibilities; he was committed and forbearing when that was prudent.

This separation of the worlds of profit and not-for-profit was largely beneficial to foundations, but much has changed since the heyday of Irwin Miller. Businesses have for their own reasons taken on social responsibilities that intersect with foundations; indeed, many businesses have foundations of their own, which want to be regarded as independent. Some are very large, as those at AT&T and Philip Morris. But their corporate/ business/stockholder self-interest and public relations are always paramount, and that makes them different from independent foundations. It is a crucial difference.

Today's corporate executive trustees usually come with MBAs, good intentions, and profit-and-loss mentalities that they want to apply to not-for-profit enterprises. Often, they fail to understand that not-for-profits have a value-laden bottom line and different purposes, that they have different priorities. Many businessmen do not understand the significance of this difference. They take Andrew Carnegie's narcissistic view that if you have built an empire of gin distilleries and car rental companies and the like, your talents are automatically transferable to the "business" of creative philanthropy. No wonder, then, that more than one senior businessman today has retired to become chairman or CEO of a foundation that he treats as a cockpit and a comfortable sinecure. The foundation's integrity loses out as a result, because foundations are completely different institutions, which require different professional capabilities.

Yet there is a persistent myth that corporate leaders and their management consultant firms have something special to offer to foundations and not-for-profits generally. Differences in purpose and potential are not appreciated. The purpose of business is to show a financial profit; the bottom line of foundations and of not-for-profits is creativity; it is to spend money well, which often involves risk taking. Fiscal management of the average business is no better than that of the average not-for-profit, but the appearance may belie reality, because businesses can operate out of the spotlight, whereas not-for-profits are always in it. Businesses are able to protect themselves from the rigors of competition by influencing legislation, lobbying for favorable administrative treatment; and when major blunders occur in automobile, banking, and aircraft institutions, government—i.e., the taxpayer—is forced to bail them out. Is there a theater, museum, research institute, scholarly organization, or laboratory that has bungled its management and fiscal affairs quite as badly as the Chrysler Corporation did? Or that has required as much of a bailout as each of the scandalous savings and loans? Can businessmen run privatized education or other public responsibilities more successfully? There is no evidence for it, and no reason why foundations should adopt the latest suspect business tactic, such as downsizing.

Business leaders and their corporations have increasingly complicated relationships with not-for-profits. Their interests may coincide, for example, in strengthening communities and their economies and making them more attractive for investment. But the collaboration can become dangerous for the weaker party if its freedom of action is hobbled. Business partners may not approve of controversial works of art, especially those brushed by the taint of eroticism or controversy. Overt "censorship" need not take place for a choice of exhibit or performance to be chilled by the interests of business board members or of a sponsoring corporation or foundation. The susceptibility of arts organizations to corporate blandishment was well illustrated by the failure of one and all to protest when a principal benefactor, Philip Morris, called on its grantees to lobby the New York City Council against legislation opposed to the interests of the tobacco giant. The oil companies, for their part, have been especially capricious supporters of not-for-profit causes, their "commitments" depending upon their year-to-year balance sheet. Few have gone to the extreme, as did ARCO, of disestablishing their entire foundation operation as part of a companywide phasing out, abruptly and utterly stranding their grantees.

Many foundation personnel as well as not-for-profit organizations hold businessmen and their practices in awe, as if they have something special to offer. Consultant gurus of the business world such as McKinsey and Peat Marwick are not the best instructors; their orientation is different from the purpose, structure, and culture of foundations and not-for-profits. William Bowen, former president of Princeton University and now president of the Mellon Foundation, an expert on organizations, has concluded that "well-regarded representatives of the business world are often surprisingly ineffective as members of nonprofit boards. . . . This harsh finding is not just my idiosyncratic view but one that is widely shared." True, nonprofit managers need better skills to manage more effectively. Toward this end, business schools should establish more differentiated training programs for not-for-profit managers.

The business executive continues to have a place on a not-for-profit board primarily because he has money and contacts and some fiscal experience to contribute, not because his profession gives him superior wisdom for what is an altogether different kind of enterprise and culture.

The role of college presidents on foundation boards, as in society, has changed. Until about twenty-five years ago, a fair number of college and university presidents were appointed to foundations primarily as leading scholars who had substantive contributions to make to the policies and program deliberations as board members. Even then, Raymond Fosdick, an estimable Rockefeller Foundation leader, was not alone in preferring no college officials on the Rockefeller board, because of their institutional agenda and his doubts about their leadership abilities. Nevertheless, college and university officials in large numbers served on foundation boards and made significant contributions to solid research and analytically oriented programs.

In the last decade, academic institutions have had to choose presidents primarily for their fund-raising abilities. Fearful of alienating large contributors, many of them have sacrificed public leadership on major issues. As *The New York Times* pointed out: "Today, almost no college or university president has spoken out significantly about Bosnia, Haiti, North Korea, health care, welfare reform, the attacks on the National Endowment for the Arts or dozens of issues high on the national agenda." Given this endemic timorousness, it is now only the exceptional university president who publicly offers something useful as a foundation trustee. And even retired college presidents have proved to be a disappointing resource. They have suffered through so many years of frustrated pleading with foundation staffs and seducing of board members that when they are appointed to a foundation board themselves, they often take the attitude that their experience has made them more knowledgeable than anyone else about how to run a foundation. The board-dominated programs in the MacArthur Foundation's first decade, for example, were significantly influenced by such agendas on the part of its retired university president trustees.

Beginning in the 1970s, the composition of independent foundation boards diversified, and their missions underwent significant changes. For the first time, boards became more reflective of society through the election of women and members of minority groups, who had been grievously underrepresented, if represented at all. Their participation has had both anticipated and quite unexpected results. As trustee agendas and deliberations are not part of the public record, it is difficult to be precise about these results except insofar as individual participants are willing to talk about them, usually off the record. The other evidences we have are the actions of trustees, as well as the foundation programs and missions that have evolved in ways that bespeak that diversity.

One immediate effect of board changes was that trustee agendas reflected more of the concerns of minority communities, with the consequent adoption of many ameliorative programs to deal with them. The effectiveness of some of these activities is in doubt, however, when they deal with symptoms, not root causes; they are benign charitable reactions, not the targeted basic research or solution-oriented activity that is the best use of adventurous philanthropy. A separate question is whether trustees who have distinct group or community interests and grievances regard their role as being largely confined to issues that affect members of minorities, or see themselves as stewards of the entire institution. There is a related question of attendance. Some trustees report that attendance at board meetings is fragmented, with some members attending only when issues that interest them are on the agenda. If true, that represents a radical departure from the fiduciary and policy responsibilities traditionally assumed by foundation board members. "We should reject categorically any notion that individual board members are meant to represent particular constituencies," wrote William Bowen, the expert on "Boardsmanship." According to recent reports, attendance has improved, possibly as the result of the winnowing out of the most egregious truants.

Other detectable changes in trustee stewardship may or may not be connected to changes in the compositions of boards. Trustees of some foundations appear to have become more directly involved in day-to-day program activities, even pressuring staffs to comply with individual trustee priorities. Whether this is the result of new activist trustee roles, or has to do with programs that appear to deal with problems in a specific locale that have profound social and political origins and impact, is not clear. What trustees favor—and what they fear—may account for outside puzzlement as to what is "in" and what is "out." For example, a project devised to inform and arouse the interest of top high school students in contemporary affairs was turned down by the Ford Foundation's Education Program because it was aimed at "elite students"—as its proposer freely admitted. This sort of elitism, he was told, could not be the purpose of a Ford Foundation program.

Deep culture and class divisions have preoccupied and distracted contemporary foundation boards. They are not bridged—they may even be exacerbated—by grantmaking that exclusively supports minority, multicultural, and intercultural activities. Both Ford and Rockefeller have chosen such a tack with their "cultural programs," and the long-term results have been mixed.

Trustees understandably like to distinguish their institutions with new program directions. The Rockefeller Foundation has long had international projects; in the 1960s its trustees created an expanded program focused on the universities and research institutions of developing countries. In the 1990s, Rockefeller president Peter Goldmark added a new dimension. He proposed to his trustees significant expenditures to promote philanthropy overseas through "foundation-like organizations." He explained: "This is not because the problems of racial injustice, disease, poverty and cultural insensitivity are so much worse abroad" but "to make the world a less parochial place. . . . Parochialism is limiting, suffocating, dangerous, and there is altogether too much of it as we lurch towards the 21st Century." The foundation, especially one of its trustees, Peggy Dulaney, took the lead in encouraging other foundations and significant donors to create foreign sources of philanthropy. Such a benevolent, idealistic rationale for making substantial U.S. philanthropic investments overseas is not greeted enthusiastically everywhere else. Vaclav Klaus, prime minister of the Czech Republic, for example, decries tax deductions for not-for-profits, calling philanthropy inherently undemocratic because it subverts the democratic inclinations of the state. And Stanley Katz of the American Council of Learned Societies has asked "whether we are sufficiently aware of the cultural differences between the donor and the donee; whether we are sure that foreign political and legal environments will not produce different philanthropic outcomes than we had intended."

The overseas card played by trustees in reaction to feared parochialism could turn out to be another kind of narrowness. There are important agendas in U.S. society that our foundations either have not tackled or have confronted only passingly. Possibly the most important impact we can have on other societies is to deal successfully with our own problems and initiate ways of contending with international ones. George F. Kennan, surely no friend of isolationism and himself a student of other societies, time and again has told us that it is how we deal with our own social and economic problems that has the greatest attractive power for friends and skeptics alike overseas.

One might gain assurance if foundation trustees opened themselves more than occasionally to the advice of knowledgeable and experienced outsiders, including critics of their activities and program plans. Instead, more foundation programs seem to be the product of trustees working with their staffs in an increasingly narcissistic atmosphere that excludes systematic consultation with relevantly experienced people outside the foundation. Such masterminding behind closed doors has frustrated those individuals and institutions that wish to be heard but are frozen out. Masterminding by trustees is also incompatible with giving generous opportunities to exceptional individuals, who have the greatest potential to lead us out of society's calamitous problems and prevent the incessant deterioration of its institutions.

To help the exceptionally qualified to achieve seemingly unattainable goals is at once a foundation's distinctive opportunity and fundamental to its existence. Only the truly venturesome will lead us to make genuine gains, sometimes through failures that yield valuable learning. Unless foundations take risks on such thinkers, researchers, and leaders, they will achieve neither success nor noble failure. Boards of independent philanthropies have immense opportunities to play critical pacesetting roles. Everything depends, first and foremost, on the caliber of trustees, their understanding of their responsibilities, and the staff leadership they select. But then stewardship of a philanthropy is not a safe harbor but rather a daily voyage into the rich possibilities of the unknown.

5

AN "UNSELFISH OCCUPATION": FOUNDATION OFFICERS, PAST AND PRESENT

As the makeup of foundation boards has changed in recent decades, so, too, have foundation staffs. Like trustees and their predecessors, many foundation administrators today differ from those of earlier times in the way that they define their role.

It is a sore point among foundation administrators that their duties are not regarded as systematic professional activity and they, therefore, are not regarded as members of a profession. That was not an issue in the past. Foundation personnel did not seek professional status because they were recruited from among recognized professionals in a discipline such as biology or political science, or as members of a profession, such as medicine, law, or environmental sciences. Virtually all came out of academic positions and held senior degrees and, frequently, tenure. Not so long ago, all officers of the Rockefeller Foundation had to have a Ph.D., and an M.D. was required of those responsible for making grants in the field of medicine. Secure in their chosen professions, they wished to be identified as a medical professional, an agricultural specialist, an economist, a political scientist, or, more rarely, a painter or playwright, rather than as the indeterminate "foundation professional." In addition to their specialty and, usually, their research experience, officers were expected to have a broad general education and wide-ranging intellectual curiosity, so that they would be conversant with the diverse backgrounds and interests of colleagues and the foundation's clients.

Today, however, advanced learning, research accomplishment, and recognized standing in a discipline or profession are rarely requirements for foundation administrators. Few are recruited from senior positions to which they can return should their foundation employment end. And the "consultants" frequently hired by foundations to run programs are often neither top scholars nor practitioners nor accomplished individuals who were tapped for their wisdom, but junior professional consultants who lack noteworthy independent track records. Hiring these part-timers for mainstream responsibilities is recent, probably borrowed from practices of the business community, where more and more part-timers and freelancers are taken on to do what full-time personnel should do, with a saving to the institution of benefits that only full-time personnel receive. Certainly, program administrators could handle more responsibilities if given adequate support staff—seemingly in short supply everywhere.

A related development is the increase in self-referential programs at foundations—programs supported by narcissistic notions rather than programs that respond to applicants, or result from commissioning qualified individuals to investigate hypotheses, or are created with strong outside expertise. This lack of vision has led to the hiring of activist program administrators, many of whom have very specific, narrow agendas for political and social change. They see themselves as having a mission, and given the general dearth of intellectual expertise and ideas among the staff, they are, as if by default, permitted to use the resources of foundations to serve their purposes. Indeed, they see this as perfectly reasonable. John E. Sawyer, then in his role as president emeritus of the Andrew W. Mellon Foundation, assessed the situation in withering terms: Foundation administrators today follow procedures that are "rigid, obscure, or bafflingly complex, sometimes leaving an impression of having been evolved more for the convenience or gratification of staff than to advance a field." Increasingly, complacent and myopic administration of foundation domain has led to the outside perception of cocksure and, not infrequently, arrogant administrators. It is the resurgence with a vengeance of Andrew Carnegie's brand of narcissistic philanthropy.

Activists can be useful goads to an establishment, whether academic or governmental or philanthropic. But to be effective provocateurs as foundation officers, they need to be multidimensional, to lend some of their activist energy to exercising insightful and mature powers of analysis and evaluation. They need to apply themselves to new subject matter, to listen and learn. Too often, they behave like Woodrow Wilson at the Paris Peace Conference, who no longer felt the need to acquire information before forming his opinions. They speak and act, and no one is apt to contradict them.

This is not to say that foundations have not had their own forms of myopia. In the past, they failed to focus on certain key social, economic, and political issues, including women's and minority rights, issues to which contemporary foundation activists give high priority. The academy is not necessarily the best source of personnel to move these issues ahead, and academics are not the only ones capable of defining or leading the way on many of the most pressing contemporary issues. But some academics and professionals with broad learning are as well qualified for these tasks as activists and certainly have something to contribute. Activist foundation officers are often self-absorbed, spending too much time seeking confirmation of their views from other foundation officers, confirmation that does not provide them with the right perspective for intellectual leadership. Nor will such officers be able to command from academia and other institutions the respect that is needed in conducting successful programs over the long haul.

Activists for social and political change may be creative as well as energetic, but are they well suited to identify and work with the most thoughtful minds among scholars and leaders who are grappling with frontier issues that affect the society as a whole? There is a difference between administrators who couple their enthusiasm for short-term projects with a manipulative power of the purse and, say, respected economists who can talk to their peers, or molecular biologists who can deal with primary issues over the long term, who know a major opportunity in a field when faced with it, who can spot it in the middistance and know what to do about it.

Today's foundation administrators are known as and pleased to call themselves "grantmakers." That title, which their predecessors would have rejected, is their common denominator; no longer are they artists or educators or biologists serving in and through foundations. The difference is that "grantmakers" primarily see themselves as handing out grants, whereas foundation officers twenty and more years ago regarded negotiating grants as only one—and far from their most important—function. They were active participants in the country's intellectual life, often as ongoing partners in cutting-edge inquiries. Primarily they were sensitive listeners who discriminated in assessing talent, who could evaluate major proposals. They helped to develop research ideas, to choose leaders of major undertakings, and then they negotiated levels of support. They did not regard themselves as superior to applicants and grantees. And rather than be tied to fixed rules, they proceeded on the basis of flexible principles. They created support structures collaboratively, to help their peers proceed intelligently and creatively with their work. The best of them were committed learners. The opportunity to learn whatever one wishes to know is, after all, the great privilege of being a foundation officer. Of course, foundation eagerness to support unusual talent in the past can be exaggerated. Trying to make this point in the 1960s, a junior Rockefeller Foundation officer proposed "Alexis de Tocqueville" for a travel grant to visit prisons in America, changing only his name but giving all his credentials; senior colleagues turned him down. The same officer proposed "Beethoven" (under another name) for a grant to write his third symphony. The application reflected the composer's life up to that time. A fabricated reference letter included called "Beethoven" intemperate and possibly gay. He was turned down. Another fake applicant was "Trotsky," writing from Mexico for funds to write a book about Stalin. Of course, he, too, bit the dust.

Today, officer involvement with grantees is often brief and perfunctory. In the past, it continued long after a grant was made, with officers extending encouragement to grantees in various ways, offering additional support, if needed, and frequently helping to build bridges to the work of others. Many traditional foundation officers were regarded by their grantees as supportive partners in research and in the work of academic and public institutions.

Contemporary foundation administrators have formed guilds, variously called "grantmakers in education" and "grantmakers in the arts," etc. These guilds are useful, chiefly to exchange information and ideas at events such as annual Council on Foundations conventions. Joint planning sessions are beneficial to their fields and for people who work in them, but they can pose dangers. A troubling example was the Independent Committee in the Arts created in the 1970s by several foundation officers, who enlisted a few high-profile artists and skilled self-publicists for input. The group was created at a time when foundation officers in the arts felt beleaguered at their respective institutions, where they faced reduced budgets and lacked attention from boards and their principal officers. Mutual commiseration evolved into an organized interest group with a barely veiled self-serving agenda; they thought to set the priorities for funding in their field, but the quality of their manifestos left much to be desired. The cardinal point is that it was an effort by a group of foundation officers—abetted by a few others, acting oligarchically—to mastermind arts and humanities policies, including funds of major foundations. The implication of such a phenomenon for prospective grantees is obvious. It was an escape from individual responsibility and threatened to create a closed shop, potentially excluding whole groups of talent while favoring others with funding. In the end, the group dissolved.

Foundation administrators acting collectively, who focus on particular ideas and even on specific people to the exclusion of others, pose a significant danger to organized philanthropy. Dean Rusk, when president of the Rockefeller Foundation, warned against such monopolistic practices. Today, it is an expression of the same narcissistic syndrome that Rusk and other past officers decried. Scholars, said Rockefeller's Warren Weaver, should not be dealt with "in the perfectly despicable manner of holding in one hand a sack of coin which you jingle and with the other hand gesturing an invitation to that scholar to work along the lines that *you* happen to think are interesting." It is one of the worst things that anybody associated with a philanthropic venture can do, if only because it is fundamentally anti-intellectual behavior. A philanthropy should be distinguished by a concern for consequential ideas and for those who originate and explicate their significance and point to their implementation. The staff's role is to be available and open to them.

Foundations today need strong leadership and staffs that are interested in ideas and in the process of arriving at them. Scientific ideas and technological advances are everywhere the center of attention, especially those that promise a speedy, practical application. Foundations working in the sciences need more farsighted science leaders like Dr. John Bowers, who was president of the Josiah Macy, Jr., Foundation for fifteen years. He had a long career in medicine, in public life, and in scholarship, sponsoring studies that focused on problems before they became pressing— ranging from medical education for women and minorities to the control of genetic engineering. Rigorous professional learning and activity led Bowers to advance these questions, not simple conjecture or idle speculation. How many foundation administrators today encourage their peers to examine the principal issues that foreseeable scientific and technological advances will impose on us?

It does not seem to be mere chance that, as long as thirty years ago, foundation leaders in the sciences such as Bowers, Weaver, and biologist Robert Morison argued for more foundation leadership in other fields, especially in the humanities. Knowledgeable foundation officers supported the American Council of Learned Societies' efforts to foster work in exotic languages that then led to systematic study of the entire culture of a nation or region. Working with university scholars, foundation officers developed new disciplines—in anthropology by the Viking Fund, in psychosomatic and social medicine by the Commonwealth Fund, in medical sociology by the Russell Sage Foundation, in higher business management by the Alfred P. Sloan Foundation. All are now firmly established disciplines whose introduction was encouraged by foundation officers with the right backgrounds and insights, who willingly explored new areas of knowledge that their university colleagues by themselves were unable or too timid to initiate. Race relations, sexual behavior, population growth, were all subjects others found too hot to handle before foundation officers (supported by their boards) took risky initiatives to support work on them.

One set of disciplines has received so little attention from foundation officers and their institutions that one is bound to ask why this is the case and how it can be changed. This is the humanities, encompassing all those disciplines from archaeology, languages, linguistics, through history and philosophy, that are ordinarily carried on in colleges and universities but have great importance way beyond their portals. As we know from earlier discussion, the humanities even today receive less than one percent of all foundation support. In the past, a portion of the problem stemmed from lack of imagination, failure to recognize that the humanities can vitally address our major problems. But one might reasonably expect present-day foundation leaders to agree that the study of man's moral relations should have high priority. Are there foundation officers who have the knowledge, nerve, and persistence to provide leadership and the means for connecting humanities scholarship to key issues? Such work needs to be carried out by exceptional humanist scholars and practitioners. Do we have foundation officers who will recognize, support, and encourage them? Part of the problem is due to accelerating foundation expenditures for mainly charitable purposes in human services to relieve the misery of those deprived of basic needs of all kinds. The problem is compounded by the fact that at present, short-term projects that attempt to achieve immediately gratifying results, are in vogue at foundations, whereas the kinds of problems that are most urgent require long-term commitments.

What then are desirable qualities in foundation officers? Foundation officers—to be responsive and discriminating in assessing proposals from whatever source—need in-depth knowledge and the intellectual capacity for learning in the fields for which they have responsibility. Without training and a substantive prior career, how can they exercise good judgment?

Intelligence, knowledge, and a capacity for learning are not enough, however, especially for evaluating and working with talented humanists and artists. Modesty, curiosity, open-mindedness, patience, imagination, and a good sense of humor are vital. A venturesome attitude—as well as a maturity some young people have and some older individuals never attain—is important. In the end, it is only by employing officers capable of making good judgments without regard to convention, people who can spot and assess the qualities of the best minds, that foundations can successfully carry out their missions and take advantage of unique investment opportunities.

Among those exceptional people, there is always one who will arrive unannounced on a foundation doorstep, or another with an unconventional background or personality, who will make unorthodox approaches. Foundation personnel must be skilled in sorting out cranks from idiosyncratic individuals who may be highly creative, who deserve to be listened to patiently and are well worth the risk of support.

Foundation officers must spend more time traveling to discover what is going on in their fields. Extensive travel experience in this society and other parts of the world is desirable in those who are recruited. As Jack Sawyer remarked: "Most fields would be better served if foundation staffs and boards recognized that the best knowledge can almost always be found 'out there.'" The demigods of efficiency, marginal savings, and speed—all virtues of commercial life—should be invoked when appropriate but should not rule over the operation in foundation work. The Rockefeller Foundation officers who discovered and granted support to well over 150 scientists, scholars, and writers who later became recipients of Nobel Prizes carried out their searches very systematically.

They made it a practice to visit repeatedly with scientists in their labs and economists in their offices and homes, with their colleagues and also their students, in the course of deciding on support for them. They talked with the potential recipients about their work and their interests, their career plans and research activities. They looked for laboratories and classrooms where young people were being inspired, their curiosity and energy provoked, in which—as one officer said—the whole was more important than the sum of its parts. In this way, the officers learned a lot more about these scholars and scientists (and about many other candidates worldwide) than they could have discovered by taking more "economic" means, with hasty single confrontations, short-term visits. This protracted process of learning firsthand holds equally true for artists in their studios and performance places. Foundation officers who travel frequently in the United States and overseas are able to establish ongoing networks of relationships, which become more valuable with time. Systematic inquiry, friendly relationships—and the time taken for these—make it possible to get to know and to distinguish the exceptional from the very good, discovering in the process the trajectory of potential recipients' career paths, what senior people think of them, what their needs are to continue their work, and whether they are innovative and original or merely interesting.

Today, too much time away from the office is spent at conferences, where foundation people encounter mainly other foundation people. Too much chumminess among foundation personnel—especially in the arts and humanities—has led to marked inbreeding, which can be corrected by the infusion of new blood and by widening the travel experience to counteract conformity and provincialism. Small cities, towns, rural areas, should be on itineraries; paradoxically, foundation officers today seem to visit more small towns in Africa than in the United States. Jet travel has shortened trips, often to one- or two-day turnarounds.

That is good for family life but not for thorough foundation work. Visits have to be sustained and repeated when significant awards are contemplated. Often, one learns what is most important through prolonged informal conversations. The pacing has to be that of the inquiring scholar rather than the salesman closing a deal on his way to the next one.

The process of learning how talented people think, how they reason, and how they operate is subtle; it takes sensitive, highly perceptive personnel, people self-confident enough to be good inquirers and listeners without feeling it is necessary to impress those they encounter with their own knowledge. It takes character and a willingness to spend the time, and finally, it takes commitment. Without such officers, foundations will have a hard time developing networks around the country or internationally to carry out their missions. There is no place on such a staff for the self-absorbed, for conventionally success-oriented people, or for those with inflexible minds.

But no matter how well prepared a staff is, if it takes chances on talent, as it should do, it will make mistakes. Some individuals will not work out. Some careers will not flourish. The failures from taking risks leave one vulnerable to criticism. It gives meaning to Warren Weaver's phrase that foundation officers have "an unselfish occupation." A story from the 1960s illustrates how one enlightened officer viewed the inherent uncertainty of this risk-taking occupation and the talent it requires. Dean Rusk at the Rockefeller Foundation was interviewing a prospective program officer, and the conversation turned to the subject of baseball. Rusk asked the young man what he thought a good batting average would be for a foundation. Perhaps considering the money and prestige of the job at stake, the candidate answered, "Probably around .750." Rusk laughed and then turned serious. If a foundation has much better than a .250 batting average, he said, he would worry it was not doing its job!

Foundation work requires determined professionals who are confident enough in their purpose to risk failure—in order to achieve great success. "The best job in the world," Harry Truman called it, when Rusk told him he was leaving the State Department to accept the presidency of the Rockefeller Foundation. And the best part of the job is the opportunity to spot and support the most creative risk takers among us.

6

THE ART OF ACTIVE
SCOUTING

Central to any grant program for individuals is the process of discovering those best qualified for support. Passive approaches,
such as bulletin board announcements and general public statements inviting applications, produce candidacies but rarely the
strongest ones. Alternatively, sitting back and waiting for candidates is simply not good enough; the talented will not reveal
themselves, at least not all and, very likely, not the best of them.

Active scouting of some kind is the answer. This is particularly true when the eligible population lives in remote rural areas
or in the inner city—areas where potential grant recipients are un-
likely to know that foundation fellowships exist; or when one is
attempting to identify young people, especially outside of the
school systems; or when one is seeking individuals with great potential who have yet to distinguish themselves; or when those eligible would not initiate applications even if they were aware of the
award program, because of time pressures, inexperience in writing
proposals, embarrassment at having to seek references from their
peers, and so forth. In general, an active search is needed when

more highly qualified candidates are desired than "open applications" of any kind produce.

Active talent scouting can take several forms: (1) by foundation staff; (2) by foundation-designated outside scouts; (3) by foundation-appointed nominators. The classic attack is for qualified foundation officers to scout and select whenever the objective is to find exceptional, mature talent or the ablest individuals in fields as diverse as biology, mathematics, physics, painting, musical composition, poetry, economics, anthropology, history, or linguistics.

The most famous foundation talent scouts were the "circuit riders" of the Rockefeller Foundation's program in the medical and natural sciences. This band of insightful and creative lookouts was gathered by Warren Weaver, who directed the program from 1932 until his retirement in 1959. Under Weaver, Rockefeller's policy was to put scientists in charge of dispensing money to scientists. Weaver was a stickler for the facts but was also a risk taker. This suited the research and fellowship program perfectly, inasmuch as the pursuit of scientific truth involves both financial and personal risk, for science patronage is a special gamble: investigators may work for years without assurance of ultimate success.

The key to Weaver's success lay in finding and appointing bold, intuitive scientists who scouted the laboratories of the world, where they made estimable selections of scientists who then received years of financial support for training and research. Weaver and his scouts brought a powerful blend of intuition, intelligence, and vision to these global searches. They not only uncovered gifted scientists—doing proud that perspicacious breed of Merton's "truffle hounds"—but also created intricate networks among the leading scientists of Europe, Asia, Australia, and the Americas. These networks included some of the most accomplished scientific research talent that could be found anywhere.

Trailing them to their laboratories, Rockefeller's people revisited the most promising of the researchers year after year. At what seemed to be a timely moment, they offered them fellowships and research opportunities to work together with leading senior scientists in their fields. But their involvement did not stop there. Contact with grantees continued indefinitely over many years; those who received support in the early stages of their careers got assistance again and again when they needed it. In turn, grantees took part in the networks that helped to identify new generations of exceptionally talented scientists.

There are many ways of measuring the success of the Rockefeller Foundation's science patronage from the early 1930s through the 1970s. Most frequently cited are the many Nobel Prizes garnered by scientists who were supported by the foundation. Through 1984, there have been sixty in Medicine, thirty-three in Chemistry, thirty-two in Physics. Over the years, many hundreds of former science and medical fellows obtained principal faculty and clinical positions in universities and research centers throughout the world and constituted a unique extended family of the foundation.

Moreover, the foundation's methodology both anticipated and directly influenced how the major governmental science patronage programs—the National Science Foundation and the National Institutes of Health—were organized. It is a clear example of a comparatively modest private-sector program establishing a pattern for originating and operating major programs with federal funds. But while Weaver's remarkably successful system has been imitated by others, it has never been matched. Similar efforts have been made in the social sciences, the humanities, and other cultural areas, but most have not been as successful.

In the 1950s and 1960s, social scientists and a few humanists were recruited by Rockefeller to scout in their disciplines. Their task was more difficult than for those in the sciences, for a number of reasons, one being that in these fields there are not the laboratories around in which scientists congregate. Moreover, standards of humanistic scholarship and artistic enterprise are not as readily measurable by objective criteria as scientific projects and their results. Nevertheless, foundation officers with professional backgrounds in the social sciences and in the humanities, acting as "circuit riders," regularly sought and discovered exceptional scholars and practitioners, in whom long-term investments were made. Evidence of their success at the Rockefeller Foundation are the twenty-nine economists and six writers who won Nobel Prizes after they had been singled out for support by the foundation, mostly early in their careers.

At one time, philanthropies had more officers with excellent scouting abilities and access to similarly astute outsiders than they do now. Any revival of distinguished individual support programs would need more "truffle hounds" and a more sophisticated network of scouts in different fields.

Outside scouts are the foundation's extended eyes and ears. Selecting these scouts is itself a demanding task for foundation personnel, requiring in-depth knowledge of subject matter and disciplines and the personnel in them. It takes keen ability to judge who has the insight and intuition for the work and how to separate out the best from the just very good. The best spotters are a rare breed, but as Merton pointed out, they are found in every walk of life, playing a role in encouraging the careers of individuals who at various developmental stages show promise of exceptional ability. They are often outstanding teachers, though they are not found only in schools and universities and teaching may not even in fact be their profession. Scouts themselves also foster excellence. They encourage maximum performance, act as catalysts to accelerate growth in others, inspire and facilitate accomplishments. In sum, they work in every way to help liberate genius. They are midwives of excellence but are not ordinarily the most accomplished professionals in their own field of scholarship or artistry; rather, they possess an uncanny ability to stimulate others to be the very best they can be. Whether serving as foundation officers or as scouts employed by foundations, they are uniquely endowed, highly creative people who understand the importance of what Professor Blackmur called the "incubation of other people," enabling them to grow.

In the arts, especially, scouts formally designated or serving informally have always played a critically important role. Composers and musicians alike regarded Nadia Boulanger as an exemplary teacher and guide possessed of astonishing intuition for recognizing exceptional musical ability in its formative stages. In theater, the late director and producer Joseph Papp had an uncanny bent for discovering promising young artists and proved it again and again. Through the theaters of his New York Shakespeare Festival, Papp was in a position to offer writers, directors, and actors the opportunity to try out their talents in protected, experimental settings. In this way, many creative individuals had their first real professional break, and confidence was instilled in them as artists at early, vulnerable stages of their careers. Lloyd Richards, at the Yale Repertory Theatre, Robert Brustein, at the American Repertory Theatre, and Gordon Davidson, at the Mark Taper Forum, also have had strong track records for finding writers and performing artists early. Their recommendations over the years proved invaluable for foundations in selecting those to support. Overseas, the spotter's role is just as important. Vice Chancellor Philip Sherlock of the University of the West Indies, for example, pointed out to visiting foundation officers the then young poet and playwright (and future Nobel laureate) Derek Walcott and the emerging literary historian Erroll Hill. Both received foundation support for their careers and for work that has enriched their students and readers. Starting in the 1950s, several large foundations began to recruit academics and administrators to represent them and manage their growing programs overseas, stationing them in key places such as Cali, Kampala, Santiago, Lagos, Mexico City. One of their chief responsibilities was to make recommendations locally for sometimes significant individual support.

By interacting with well-positioned persons in the humanities, and even more in the arts in the United States, the Ford Foundation's cultural program had its greatest impact under the leadership of W. McNeil Lowry. Lowry was to the identification of arts talent what Warren Weaver was to science. He spotted key leaders on which the Ford Foundation built major performing arts institutions in theater, ballet, and music in every region and in many cities nationwide in the 1950s and 1960s. Lowry recruited such artists as the violinist Isaac Stern and the theater director Alan Schneider to assist him in finding upcoming artists, whom Lowry then supported through Ford's programs. The late Lincoln Kirstein, himself one of the country's leading patrons of the arts, called Lowry "the single most influential patron of the performing arts the American democratic system has ever produced." In the course of the efforts to guide communities in building significant arts institutions with Ford Foundation support, Lowry raised the public's consciousness, its fundamental understanding of the arts and their importance. He never wavered in his conviction that a private foundation's fundamental task is to find and nurture the exceptional individual. Just before his death in 1992, Lowry said: "Like any other agency, public or private, the Foundation can learn enough about the arts to recognize that it has only one wager it can make with conviction and that is the wager on individual talent, whether that talent creates a loom or provides direction for an institution or group." Peter Zeisler, longtime head of the not-for-profit professional organization the Theatre Communications Group, and a Lowry protégé, stated it accurately:

"Mac's success as a philanthropist was due to his uncanny ability to listen. A fierce believer in the vision of the artist, Mac invested his money in people." It is unfortunate that Lowry's voice is no longer heard.

The scope and purpose of programs aimed at nurturing top talent are few and are usually limited to a single subject, sometimes to a field. Some examples in diverse disciplines are the Klingenstein Foundation's program for investigators in the neurosciences, the Sloan Foundation's programs for scientists and economists, the Whiting Foundation's and Lila Wallace Fund's programs for writers. The MacArthur Prize Fellows Program is, in principle, an exception. It also has a specific purpose but a most adventurous one—the long-term support of exceptionally talented individuals—and candidates in all disciplines and fields are eligible. But in MacArthur's Prize Fellows Program, too, there is a strong emphasis on political correctness and themes in awards, especially in the arts and humanities.

Programs like MacArthur's use nominators, the third of the three methods of active scouting for talent. Nominators filter candidates qualitatively while immediately limiting the numbers that will be considered. Without active screening, officers would be deluged by applications, effectively preventing both the staff and the program's selection committee from giving due time and attention to the best-qualified candidates. Nominators are experts in or at least keen observers of a program's field or fields. They propose the candidates to be selected by a committee charged with selecting a predetermined number of awards. There may be fifty or a hundred nominators (roughly one hundred is the number currently used by Wallace, MacArthur, Whiting), distributed geographically and in different parts of a field's spectrum—e.g., fiction, poetry, playwriting, etc. Nominators may be asked to propose one candidate in a program year or several and are sometimes, but not often, paid. Usually they are appointed for one year at a time and serve anonymously, but in some programs their names are made public late in the selection process.

Most programs using nominators and a selection committee offer a specific number of awards and are competitive—that is, award recipients are chosen annually on a comparative basis. There are some exceptions. The MacArthur program was a "rolling" one at the outset, with no deadlines and no specific number of awards. The selection committee recommended to the board twenty to thirty recipients at a time, on a noncompetitive basis. The procedure changed five years into the program, when the board imposed a restricted annual budget. That put a ceiling on awards, which meant that only a limited number could be recommended—once a year on a competitive basis. Thus competition among candidates was forced on the program, producing a radical change in its purpose and style.

The antecedent to MacArthur's "rolling" program was the Imaginative Writing and Literary Scholarship Program at the Rockefeller Foundation in the 1960s. For five years, an extraordinary group of writers met every eight to ten weeks to discuss the work of writers proposed by an annually changing group of nominators selected by them and the staff. The writers on the selection committee served anonymously and recommended awards from time to time, based on their evaluations of an individual candidate's work. Initially, the committee comprised Saul Bellow, Stanley Kunitz, and Robert Lowell. In succeeding years, Robert Penn Warren, Walker Percy, John Hersey, James Dickey, were added. Young writers—Jean Valentine, Frank Conroy, and Robert Coles—joined the group toward the end of the program's five-year-run, in 1969. The process and the grants constituted an exercise in quality that became a model for the writers' programs at the Whiting, Lila Wallace, and Lannan foundations, as well as, procedurally, for MacArthur's Prize Fellows Program.

Among high-quality individual grant programs, the notable

exception to private foundation programs using nominators is the Guggenheim, to which anyone may apply. In the past, careful staff procedures there took care of the quality problem, directing the selection committee's attention to those most qualified for consideration. In this way, the working numbers were drastically reduced to a manageable total. However, any selection committee member could initiate full consideration of any applicant.

Under the present administration, some Guggenheim recipients can be recommended for awards by experts in their field. But the entire field is sifted by committees, until the final selection committee members deal with several thousand candidates en route to decisions. The Guggenheim standards are unquestionably high, but one has to wonder if unusual first-rate candidates are not lost among thousands of direct applicants.

The exemplar of any profession using scouting and selection procedures is baseball.

The clubs' methods of appraising, nurturing, and advancing players could provide very useful pointers to foundations. All major-league teams have active, full-time talent scouts. They do not confine themselves to studying averages in *The Sporting News* or to following up on those whose pitching and batting prowess has already brought them to prominence among professionals. Instead, major-league scouts crisscross the nation, visiting prospects in colleges, on sandlots, in the semipro and the minor leagues. They talk with high school coaches—even in the smallest towns— and can be found in the stands at inner-city games. They listen to the wisdom and the gossip in clubhouses and hotel lobbies and follow up leads on players in games sponsored by the American Legion and a host of other such civic organizations. They have international scouting networks covering Japan, Central America, and, undeterred by political problems, Cuba.

Baseball scouts are carefully chosen by professional management. Many are themselves former players, but none are mere retreads; their role is too important for them to be anything less than experts. Scouts must be able to extrapolate potential talent from among the ranks of untrained youngsters whose development they follow from year to year and place to place. They get to know the promising players and their families, give encouragement and advice, and report the youngsters' progress to their home offices. Some teams even employ "cross-checkers," senior scouts who are sent out to make sure that the original reports on a prospect are accurate.

Every baseball scout would like to be the first to discover a natural talent who bats, throws, and fields like Joe DiMaggio or pitches like Sandy Koufax. When scouts encounter a young Willie Mays or Tom Seaver, their main effort is to keep him away from those who might spoil his natural abilities. Scouts find that most of the outstanding prospects need gradual, consistent coaching and encouragement, with attention given to their personal maturation as well as to the stretching and refining of their playing skills. Scouts must therefore be nurturers, or at least know what nurturing needs to be done and who can best be entrusted with the task.

Minor-league managers, coaches, and scouts strive to place prospects with the most appropriate coaches in each team's farm system. These nurturing managers and coaches are integral to developing skills and encouraging personal growth, which, aided by the passage of time, determine when a young talent is ready for major-league baseball. Most do not make it.

Professional baseball invests heavily in its scouting and farm system. It is the research and development arm that perpetuates the sport, and teams compete to employ the best selectors and nurturers. The franchises take major financial risks on those players most likely to break into major-league ranks, as well as on those whose futures are less certain and who may never be of major-league caliber. Whether these players "make it" or not, they are not regarded as failures of the scouting and nurturing system. The unpredictability of scouting is accepted, even deemed necessary, as part of a system prepared to make significant investments because the goal—a winning and profitable team—is worth the risks.

So it is, too, for philanthropies, except that the stakes are higher, with the added value that a potentially significant contribution to the larger world may result from such an investment. To find and deal with exceptional individuals, a foundation itself must be creative. Its search and selection procedures must evolve from conceptions of excellence that go beyond conventional notions of imaginative ideas and creativity for a moral, human purpose. Foundations must be open to bold ideas, welcome the unconventional, listen to what may be unsettling, because it is different and new and speaks to quality. The most exceptional talent is almost never the most obvious.

7

CHARACTERISTICS OF THE CREATIVE AND TALENTED

The characteristics of exceptional individuals cannot be easily defined; there is no single type and therefore no typology. Originality is perhaps the common denominator among the exceptionally talented, but originality and corollary characteristics manifest themselves in different ways. Scouts for talent are not primarily concerned with raw capacities except when they are working through programs for schoolchildren. They are most interested in the interrelationship of characteristics and demonstrated ability in particular individuals and what their achievements say about the likelihood of their continued growth and creativity.

Except in the hard sciences, distinguishing inimitable talents from those who are simply very good is difficult. As the planners of the MacArthur Prize Fellowships recognized, our time is not one that values individual initiative. "Rugged individualism" is not genuinely valued outside the business world, and the term "elite" raises the ire of religious leaders, academics, and politicians. Exceptional individual achievements are usually homogenized; the achievers are buried in groups and committees. Highest marks in our society are given for group cooperation rather than for individual imagination or achievement.

How then do we recognize the creative and original thinkers among us? Robert J. Sternberg has compiled a list of cognitive characteristics that set the best apart. In his book *In the Nature of Creativity*, Sternberg distilled the writings of such fellow psychologists as David Feldman and Mihaly Csikszentmihalyi— as well as Howard Gardner and David Perkins, the principal investigators at Harvard's Project Zero, where research on the nature of creativity is going on—to arrive at a profile of the gifted individual. In addition to originality, high intelligence is a common denominator, but there are many forms of intelligence. Only a few forms are easily identifiable; fewer are measurable. More apparent characteristics are imagination, creativity, and logical reasoning capacity. Sternberg found that exceptional individuals have high intrinsic motivation. That is, they are motivated by interest, enjoyment, and satisfaction in the work itself, and also by a willingness to take risks, to face adversity. They are generally free spirits who set their own rules, seek the unusual, are unconventional and open to new experiences. Most are task-focused and persevering.

Sternberg's book showed that highly gifted individuals are unusually prone to suffer from stress. They experience tension between their need for independence and privacy and their desire for acceptance and praise. Different sometimes to the point of idiosyncratic, they may be shunned and forced into isolation. Their quests are often lonely, single-minded ones. And this isolation and single-mindedness may make them appear egotistical, a frequent accusation leveled against "the elite." What keeps them going despite these handicaps and the usual false starts is a value-shaping vision that justifies itself and sustains them, and the praise and support they receive, which keeps the creative process alive.

Foundation officers capable of recognizing talent should be directly addressing these needs.

Foundation officers need to be alert to all kinds of intellectual textures among talented individuals. This is difficult, especially when it comes to identifying and nurturing those who will create important new art. Art, as well as the artist, is often contentious initially, hard to understand, to validate, to defend—in a word, it is often alienating. The general public does not initially see innovative art—such as the Impressionists' paintings of the 1870—as beautiful. Critics and politicians who dominate the system at any time tend to be defensive, outraged, and censorious when they first confront challenging innovation. To further complicate the issue, lay people often have difficulty distinguishing between artistic originality and sheer trendiness, as, for example, with the photographer Robert Mapplethorpe. Foundation officers and the panels they appoint, too, may mistake the one for the other. The NEA got itself into serious trouble with Congress and gave an opening to its ideological enemies on the right by supporting exhibitionism posing as art, which moreover struck many people as offensive.

Artists are their own primary support system, and keeping the dynamic visionary impulse of genuine artists alive demands considerable courage. It takes the responsible support of others, however, to keep their hopes and enthusiasm for their work alive, to "maintain the spirit of pure inquiry and curiosity about life and our culture," as the sculptor Leonard Hunter said. Just as the humanist's challenge to the values and moral sense of his time is vital to a healthy society, so, too, is the artist's curiosity to create in new ways, his commitment to taking creative risks, his courage to be an outsider, to sometimes fail in order to get ahead—all precious American virtues worthy of support.

Among talents, those that contribute to leadership ability are the most difficult to define, but they are of such importance at every level of society that cultivating exceptional leadership talent deserves a high priority. There are several foundation programs that nurture the particular kinds of leadership that will direct major public programs and institutions in the United States and abroad. These programs, like those fostering the careers of scientists, scholars, and artists, look for exceptional talents in order to aid in their development. But leadership talent manifests itself differently, can be harder to spot, and requires unique support efforts. One of the most interesting of these efforts was started in 1980 by the W. K. Kellogg Foundation; it gives three-year fellowships annually to as many as fifty individuals who already have academic or public-service or cultural careers. Their fellowships are structured to enable them to gain "a broader knowledge and experience base" that takes them "beyond the confines of their chosen careers." Each fellow's program is partly self-directed, partly conducted as a group in seminars in America and abroad. It is an expensive program and highly competitive (in 1994, 597 applicants were screened down to 132, who were then interviewed by the foundation to select 25 women and 25 men). The Kellogg Foundation justifies this investment in young professionals as having "the greatest possibility for improving the human condition."

The Ashoka Foundation is an international program that seeks out leadership talent to work on key social issues. Ashoka (Sanskrit for "absence of remorse") was created by a remarkable, innovative leader, William Drayton, to find and support social entrepreneurs in their own countries. By 1995, Ashoka had recruited six hundred people with new ideas, who set out to change some important area of social life. Given modest means to carry out their ideas—in education or environmental protection, for example—Ashoka fellows at the beginning of 1995 were active in twenty-one countries in Asia, Africa, and Latin America.

Through contacts among the social entrepreneurs, their innovations can proliferate.

To understand what talent and what standards Ashoka aims for, and why, one needs to know that the six hundred active fellows are chosen by panels of fellows themselves. There are no age, background, or ideological limitations. To be chosen, a candidate must be innovative and creative, must put forward a realistic proposal to implement social changes of lasting importance on a national or international level. Ashoka's effectiveness has attracted supplementary funding from a large number of foundations and corporations.

The Harkness Fellowship program of the Commonwealth Fund offers emerging leaders in the United Kingdom, Australia, and New Zealand a year's opportunity to study a particular problem or situation in the United States. Formerly intended for outstanding U.K. graduate students, the program was reorganized a few years ago. The new focus is on people in midcareer who treat America as a crucible for learning about government and community work on shared public issues, such as health care, education, and addiction. Harkness's director, Keith Kirby, a Briton admits that leadership development is a difficult notion. "It sounds elitist," but as the competition is "to choose the best possible people," elitism, says Kirby, is an accurate term. Successful candidates must have "a vision relevant to the great issues of the day" and will go home as innovators, as opinionmakers, as leaders—as "agents of change."

The Harkness selection system tends toward the cautious, though less conventional persons are sought too. Kirby recognizes that mavericks may be innovators who will enrich the Harkness program by shaking up routine attitudes and viewpoints. Mavericks may have unusual career paths, often with unexplained discontinuities that corroborate Kirby's belief that "the ladder of success need not be linear." The way Kirby finds constructive mavericks for the Harkness program is to deemphasize interviews and written applications. Instead, Kirby learns about them by closely questioning their references. He is convinced that this broader net brings in a rich diversity of people.

In philanthropy, as in architecture, form must follow function. If the purpose is to reward an individual because he or she is the best in a field or profession—a prize for the leading cancer researcher, for example—then the criteria have to include some concept of what constitutes the best in that field. If, however, the aim is to support outstanding upcoming talent in a field—a cultural historian, say, who exhibits great promise for someday becoming one of the best—then potential recipients must be judged by the highest standards of historical scholarship and assessed for likely further talent development. The criteria are different again for selecting the right individual to accomplish a specific project—say, an economist working on a comparative analysis of housing costs in New York and Detroit. The question then becomes: What are his or her professional qualifications for this specific piece of work? The selection criteria for leadership talent and potential— best suited to the Kellogg, Ashoka, and Harkness programs—are diverse, but each is also specific.

While developing leadership talents are the most difficult to identify and select, the second most difficult individuals to spot are those who bring exceptional capacities to an important field of investigation, such as the study of genetic influences on behavior, or to a critical problem, such as nuclear weapons proliferation. Finding and supporting such people is a principal responsibility of foundations. The criteria for selection of these individuals and for creating systemic support systems for them involve knowledge and intuition, confidence and risk taking. Who is eligible for consideration and who for support, and at what career stage? Based on what evidence of past accomplishment or future potential are selections to be made? Is there a value-added factor that can be employed in distinguishing among those eligible for support? Is this the right time to make an investment that will enable a prospective recipient to make a significant leap forward in his or her work or to make an important career change? Given the assurance of sustained support, would an individual try something that he or she could not otherwise do, or might not even have thought of? Would the award be used to move into a new field or to work collaboratively with others in different fields? Or would it be used to go "into residence" at an institution to learn from its give-and-take, perhaps to make discoveries and be inspired by completely new kinds of energies?

The value-added concept justifies taking greater risks because there is a chance of making a significant breakthrough in the careers of exceptionally creative individuals. A value-added grant may single out talented people for recognition, for attention and encouragement, for financial and other sustaining support, at the most vulnerable point in their careers. And from this emerges the most important criterion in making such grants: The awards should go to those for whom recognition and support will make the *most* difference. The awarding foundation, therefore, has to examine several elements before making its selection:

- Evidence of accomplishment of work of the highest quality;
- Evidence of commitment to the work;
- Likelihood of continued significant achievement; and
- Potential for value-added accomplishment as a consequence of the award.

Candidates for such affirming support at the emergent stage of their careers must have demonstrated early on that they have staying power. Their past achievements are the principal indicators of likely future accomplishments; demonstrated excellence justifies anticipating more of the same. Awards given early in a career are especially coveted and afford foundations the opportunity to play a nurturing role rivaling the importance of their financial support.

A foundation must be explicit about defining its terms for exceptional individuals. The term "emerging talent" does not by itself make clear whom the foundation is looking for. Age may or may not be relevant. The emerging female fiction writer or scholar, for instance, may be a woman in her early forties or older who has turned to professional pursuits after years devoted to rearing children. Dancers and mathematicians, on the other hand, emerge in their teens or not at all. The talents of painters and sculptors are different yet again, usually taking longer to blossom than those of composers and writers. There are typical patterns in other professions. Physicists ordinarily succeed at an earlier age than social scientists, who acquire their particular experience over a longer time, and a playwright in midcareer is likely to have had more productions than a poet of the same age has published books. Thus age as a factor needs to be tempered by an understanding of respective professional requirements and by individual career choices, especially by women.

Professionals in midcareer are a different group but no less important as candidates for support. They are the scientists, artists, and scholars who have demonstrated an ability to do the work and who are productive. Few have received much recognition for their work or have enjoyed free time to work independently to this point. Therefore, midcareer is often a launching point for a new level or kind of work, or an opportune moment for a change in specialties. Grants can relieve these professionals of economic pressures, enabling them to achieve serious growth. Virtually all need funds, above all to buy the gift of unencumbered time.

At what point in a selection process should financial need become a consideration? Financial criteria can be more easily declared than measured. For support at a value-added level, financial need is not an appropriate criterion in the selection process until candidates are winnowed on the basis of the quality of their work and what that work says about their likely achievements in the future.

In the best situations, selection committees should be encouraged to take risks in assessing the characteristics of candidates for support. Their charge to recommend those who are most able may, in some instances, cause them to include those who are most likely to break ranks, "to make something happen." Those best situations, however, do not come easily.

8

SELECTING THE TALENTED: PANELS, COMMITTEES, AND PROCEDURES

The first and longtime president of the John Simon Guggenheim Foundation, Henry Allen Moe, wrote near the end of a remarkably successful career that "the choosing of persons is a creative art in which the subliminal, as in all creative arts, is the most important part—the subliminal self employing the materials gathered by the work-a-day consciousness." It is an eloquent statement that elevates the whole business of singling out unusual talent to an art, doing justice to an enterprise that is the persistent theme of this book. But Moe's statement does not, by itself, help the uninitiated to understand how on a practical level foundations decide who should be supported.

Systematic individual support programs in which nominees or applicants vie for a limited number of awards typically employ selection committees. They are usually small, five to seven members (always uneven numbers to avoid a hung jury), or are larger, as at the NEA, where there may be fifteen or more on a panel. Foundation staff members usually recruit selectors for their expertise, and sometimes their choices need to be ratified by the foundation's trustees. The choice of a selection committee is critical and must be thoroughly thought out, with potential problems carefully negotiated, for the group to work smoothly together. While knowledge and experience are obviously the key factors in choosing selectors, their personal characteristics may be almost as important. One wants individuals who have sufficient knowledge to make rigorous judgments, but one wants them also to be generous and imaginative, open-minded, seasoned, and perspicacious.

Individual selectors need to be able to work well with committee colleagues. But to work well as a member of a group does not mean acquiescing to the majority around the table; in fact, submissive people make unhelpful committee members, because they become a drag on the consensus. Conversely, highly assertive individuals are counterproductive, because their forcefulness typically is at the expense of listening to their colleagues' arguments. While one would like the leaders in a given field to be included in selection committees, it should be kept in mind that there are people renowned for scholarship or creativity who are not at their best working in a group. Alternatively, some lesser-known people in the same field may have a superior ability to work with others in arriving at the same high-standard judgments.

It makes a qualitative difference in the end result whether an awards panel or a selection committee meets just once or does its job over time. Perhaps it does not matter so much for deliberations leading to the award of a lesser prize—for that, a selection group may reach a satisfactory result in only one meeting. But for major awards that can make an important difference in the careers of winners (and losers)—such as, in the literary field, the Pulitzer Prize and the National Book Award—a single, brief meeting by their committees does not do justice to the purpose. Too much is at stake.

My experience with programs in a variety of fields—three at the Rockefeller Foundation, and at MacArthur, Whiting, and the Rona Jaffe Foundation—has shown the effectiveness of multiple

meetings by a small selection group. Committee members get to know and trust one another and will listen to debate on the issues involved in giving full consideration to candidates and to their work. Participants in such thorough, sustained selection processes themselves invariably believe they lead to better results, and are more pleased with the process and the outcome than with those of one-shot decision meetings.

Through the 1960s, most selection committees worked in the sustained fashion, such as those for the Legal and Political Studies Program and the International Relations Program, whose committees included such distinguished figures as Judge Philip Jessup of the World Court, Hans Morgenthau of the University of Chicago, Robert Scalapino of Berkeley, and Robert Bowie of Harvard's Center of International Affairs, who was director of the State Department's Policy Planning Staff. These were all very busy people, but they read voluminously and met repeatedly. Despite computers and other labor-saving technology, not many of today's intellectuals and officials have sufficient time for prolonged service of this kind, though programs that insist on it can still find willing individuals who are qualified. Originally, the MacArthur Foundation's selection committee had more than twenty members—some of the country's leading scholars, writers, and administrators—who attended two-day meetings monthly in Chicago and read substantial dossiers in between. Their virtually flawless attendance records make these marathons even more impressive. The committee was, however, too large for easy exchanges across the table, and the participation of half a dozen of the foundation's board members—some of whom tended to dominate—was a mistake, which has since been corrected.

One selection committee configuration that works well is convened for a series of annual Whiting Writers Awards, ten $30,000 grants given to writers near the beginning stages of their careers. A new group of nominators annually produces the pool of about one hundred candidates. The committee of five to six writers and editors, which revolves annually, meets up to four times over about eight months to discuss the works of the nominees, whom they have read extensively. The discussions lead to gradual winnowing of the list. Short-list candidates (which may number up to twenty-five) are discussed at least twice before recommendations of awards are made by consensus. The frequency of meetings makes for both informality and directness of discussion, and because participants are encouraged to put all their cards on the table and know they operate with complete confidentiality, there is a minimum of academic or literary politics.

Of course, the makeup of any committee is key to its success. The inclusion of both men and women, of people from different parts of the geographic and intellectual/artistic spectrum of the subject, is vitally important, but the involvement of superior and fair-minded individuals obviates the need for quotas of any kind. As selectors are often at their best after a year or two of experience with the program and each other, it is often advantageous to have some holdovers from year to year, although the overall panel should change annually. Finally, it make sense for the committee's chair to be a foundation officer rather than a selector. But while the chair may advance questions and move the discussion along, he or she does not participate in building a consensus and does not cast a vote.

In programs where foundation officers make decisions without benefit of a selection committee, they usually solicit judgments from colleagues, critics, reviewers, and scholars, including those proposed by the candidates. Most of these judgments are useful more to fill a file and buttress a case than to make the decision. One reason for this is that references often waffle now that technology makes letters of recommendation less likely to remain confidential. Some referees try to second-guess what the foundation or its corresponding program officer wants to hear. Sometimes enlightening evaluations that are also trustworthy come in, but the reference letter scene, all in all, is a sorry one. As Warren Weaver said: "I have the highest disrespect for letters of recommendation." At the MacArthur Foundation, in the early years of the Prize Fellows Program, twelve to fifteen reference letters were solicited for each candidate. Those evaluations useful to the committee were often the ones that were supplemented by telephone inquiries, during which referees would become more enlightening under questioning. While telephone references are more reliable than written ones, these, too, have diminished in candor in an age of surreptitious listening and tampering. It is also important that sensitivity be exercised in soliciting references. A leading American composer, the head of a major conservatory, was asked by the MacArthur Prize Fellows staff to act as a reference for a bright young composer nominee. With a candor foundations rarely experience, the senior composer exploded with anger, demanding whether the foundation understood how critically important five years of generous support would be for a composer like himself, who had never had such an opportunity, and reproaching them for their cruelty in asking him to supply a reference for a composer with less than half his own experience. Senior people cannot always be spared such indignity, but clearly foundations need administrators sensitive to the feelings of creative people, who are usually not in a position to speak out for themselves.

Nominators of candidates, when well chosen, perform a valuable service. Professionals and keen observers in a program's field, they have the contacts not only at established institutions but perhaps also with grassroots groups, dissidents within the discipline, and other minorities. Ideally, said Robert Merton, they "have an eye for seeing talent of various kinds before this has become apparent to everyone else . . . men and women who somehow see below the surface of appearance to underlying quality, who somehow know excellence when they first encounter it, and before others are cognizant of it." The use of nominators may not be democratic, but then the search for "the best" is not an egalitarian or a populist exercise.

There is some controversy over whether nominators and selection committees should be paid. Historically, leaders in a field regarded their service as a contribution of professional time. They expected only to have expenses paid and were pleased to assist a grantmaking foundation working in their field and to have the ego satisfaction of participating in an important decision. It appears this ethic no longer predominates. Nominators almost certainly do not need to be paid. The MacArthur Foundation's nominators, who were paid, said when polled that they would have been pleased to help without recompense. Selectors are a different case. In principle, it seems appropriate to pay those who are asked to spend much time reviewing and discussing candidates, attending several meetings. Think, for example, of the effort required to consider the two hundred–odd manuscripts for a writing program like Whiting's and the even larger number of manuscripts, slides, and scores reviewed by Guggenheim's selectors. Where made, payments usually do not adequately compensate for actual time spent, yet they should be more than a token. But no more than a modest fee is expected, and if more than that were paid, selectors might serve for the wrong reasons.

Foundations have to be careful not to recruit selectors in the same field who are current or potential applicants for the foundation's support. Sometimes foundations have made the mistake of recruiting their own grantees for such service as a virtual quid pro quo. Above all, one has to be careful to exclude those apt to use their position as selectors to lobby for a particular point of view or to reward or punish colleagues in the field. Yet it happens. Even then, of course, it makes a difference if the lobbying takes the form of advocacy for rather than political opposition to a candidate.

Individual grant programs such as Wallace and MacArthur

have high public visibility. That puts nominators, selectors, and referees who are asked to serve them under special pressure. They want to be in good standing for their own future support needs and, to that end, try to show their affinity with the officers' aims. For some, that means coming up with whatever they think the foundation wants to hear; or coming up with candidate characteristics the foundation seems to want—as exemplified by the past record of awards. Some nominators and referees undoubtedly do this subconsciously; others do it knowingly. For example, a few nominators and several referees frequently used by MacArthur complained to former program officers in the mid-1980s that the program's quality was eroding, its leadership fumbling, the quality of the candidates they were asked to comment on low. They said they wished to quit serving the program, but they did not, presumably because they did not want to reduce their own chances of one day receiving a Prize Fellowship. There was also the excitement of participating in a program that received so much media attention.

Media interest puts program participants under special pressure to maintain confidentiality to protect the candidates. Sensitive information that comes to light is protected most of the time, but not always. Breaches of confidence, whether as a result of error or insensitivity, and whether or not they have consequences, are unacceptable. Word of lapses gets around fast and shakes the confidence of scholars and others on whose collaboration a foundation depends.

Confidentiality is required throughout the screening process, not for its own sake but because there has to be sensitive regard for individuals whose hopes and aspirations are at stake. For example, one always stresses to new selection committee participants that they have a special responsibility not to reveal who their fellow members are. Despite this, one member of the MacArthur selection committee in the first year ennobled himself at a dinner party by revealing to a rapt audience the names of the distinguished other members. Hearing this, one committee colleague threatened to quit. A *New York Times* correspondent also learned the names of those on the committee, but the foundation persuaded her not to publish them. Such breaches are infrequent; the overwhelming majority who serve take their obligations seriously.

Another controversial issue is whether nominators should be identified publicly by the foundation. The principal reason for their serving anonymously is to protect them from being pressured by candidates and their adherents and other aspirants. Such "secret" service has been criticized, however. A system of open results secretly arrived at does not sit well with the thwarted legions who cannot apply and cannot be given the names of nominators they would like to propose them. Foundation programs that operate this way receive many pleading letters from frustrated hopefuls. These importunities should always be responded to politely and firmly, the foundation's processes and policies explained (some foundations do not do this, a signal failing). Yet there will always be some who call the process undemocratic, which it has to be because of its purpose; and some who call it unfair, which it is not, given its purpose.

As a result of outside pressures, some foundations reveal the names of their selection committee members when the awards are announced or in their annual reports. Ideally, this should not happen until long after the awards have been given, if at all, so that there is no effect—not even a subconscious one—on the selectors' decisions. One wonders, however, how long the lid can be kept on in a society that equates public revelation with virtue. After all, the media succeed in charging into the most private concerns; why then should interested parties not demand to be spectators at a fellowship selection meeting?

The debate over anonymous service by nominators and selectors is but one element in the larger controversy of "open" versus "confidential" or "secret" selection procedures. Application versus nomination is often a central issue. How should candidacies be brought forward? Should candidates themselves be active participants in the process? There is no single right way to structure such programs, and no true marriage of excellence and program formula has been devised. Trying out new ideas should be encouraged. (An innovative program of selective nomination that also permits direct application was adopted by the Massachusetts Council on the Arts in the late 1980s, but it was stopped when the legislature eliminated the council's funding as a result of the state's fiscal crisis.)

A significant advantage of the selective nomination system, as we have seen, is that it provides more control over the many procedures involved and enables a foundation to focus sharply on the purpose of its program. The principal disadvantage of this technique is that it is perceived as unfair because of the aura of secrecy, which causes some to suspect that the only candidates proposed are personal favorites, those whom decisionmakers already know and wish to advance. Programs with only a few recipients are especially susceptible to suspicions of favoritism. These suspicions are probably unwarranted, but that is not the main point. Programs need to be conducted in a proper and fair manner, as well as in a manner *perceived* to be both proper and fair.

The most controversial "secret" procedures are in programs where candidates are nominated and considered for support without their participation and often without their knowledge. Typically under such programs, individual candidates are not notified unless they are successful at the conclusion of the process. The unsuccessful candidates are usually not contacted at all and may never know that they were considered. Although controversial, these procedures are completely justifiable. One wants to avoid raising the hopes of many candidates when only a few will succeed. Moreover, contact with candidates is often irrelevant to the process, as, for example, in programs for artists where the selections are based exclusively on judgments of their past work.

Until 1987, when the tax law was changed, one reason for not involving candidates was that grants and fellowships were regarded as tax-free "prizes," provided their recipients did not participate in the selection process and were under no obligation to perform services in return for their award. One hopes that the exemption will one day be reinstated. Keeping candidates uninvolved also simplifies matters for the grant program staff, reduces costs, and decreases the possibility that the selection process will be influenced by extraneous personal matters.

Although such programs are well established by now, and their confidential selection procedures widely accepted, they are still subjected to some criticism because there is no opportunity for potential candidates to apply. And because candidates have no opportunity ordinarily to put their best foot forward with a written submission, the foundation is thereby confined to deciding on the basis of information received from nominators and whatever other sources are consulted. There are experienced observers who feel that in some programs, candidates should be interviewed, especially where the proffered support is extremely generous and extended over time, so as to make a very substantial difference in each recipient's career. A sign of the times is the increasing number of critics who believe that current procedures coddle candidates needlessly by guarding them against disappointment.

However, in the planning discussions of the MacArthur Foundation, some members of the board went so far as to say that written applications or interviews would unfairly benefit articulate candidates. Others argued that the fellowship's size and prestige made it important that candidates who reached the final decision stage be interviewed. They felt that without an interview or at least a detailed statement of plans, the unknown, the young, and the mavericks would be at a decided disadvantage, in a program ostensibly intended to include such individuals. Candidacies could be treated confidentially until the ultimate stage, when finalists could be interviewed or invited to submit a written work plan. After 1987, the tax exemption of the awards was no longer an inhibition to this. At one point, board members seemed to be won over, in principle, to interviewing candidates. However, selection committee members said they were too busy to participate and did not want to entrust the staff with the responsibility. Then Jonas Salk, a selection committee member, inadvertently created a problem by generously volunteering to interview the candidates on behalf of the committee. They were not prepared to give one of their number that much power and decided against interviewing anybody. Yet no matter how many references are solicited on each candidate's behalf, significant information about some individuals and their work plans that should be factored into the foundation's decision—information that only the candidates themselves can provide—remains unavailable.

Although a selection system should always attempt to be thorough and fair, some foundations seem to have made a virtual fetish of creating supposed "equalities" in procedures, the results of which may be quite different from what is intended. Not all procedures inspired by a foundation officer's passion for fairness have the best effect. Some individual grant programs for artists, especially those at state agencies and the NEA, consider candidates "blind"—i.e., panelists do not know whose poems they are reading or whose music they are hearing. That approach seems "fair," but in fact candidates may get more thorough consideration if it is known who they are, where they are in their career, what their past accomplishments are, etc. Moreover, some panelists are able to recognize an artist by his or her style, which means that those more knowledgeable panelists may not in fact be making "blind" assessments at all.

Another misguided practice intended to ensure "fairness"—one that is also used in the NEA's literature program—is the requirement that panelists write five lines about each candidate they review. (They are not allowed to fill up the five lines with the words "bad, bad, bad, bad"!) Pity the poor panelists who in 1995, for example, each had four hundred poets to assess. Further, it is assumed by foundations that for fairness' sake, if one candidate is interviewed in a competitive situation, all others must be interviewed. But this is not necessarily so. The objective is to get sufficient information to make a proper evaluation and high-standard decision on each candidate. It may prove necessary, therefore, to interview some people because the selectors have not learned enough about them, though they already possess sufficient data about others.

Timing of an award is a particularly crucial concern, or should be, and is a valid reason for interviewing in some cases. Is this the right moment for a particular scholar or professional or artist to be freed of money-making obligations, to have free time, to be taken out of his or her classroom, studio, or laboratory? Or is it premature (or perhaps too late)? The timing factor is probably the one least well judged by foundation officers, especially when they do not have direct contact with the candidates. It is a difficult assessment, takes discernment, imagination, and subtlety, and is most likely to be weighed properly in the course of direct discussion. This is, of course, especially important with a major long-term award. Polished competitive people may get more attention from direct contact with foundation officers than they need, but the unusual individual, or the reticent introvert who does not know how properly to represent himself, may get a more informed and sympathetic hearing this way.

Overall, the refusal to interview candidates is part of the depersonalization of selection procedures that seems to be on the rise everywhere (for example, in college and graduate school admissions). At foundations, it is part and parcel of a greater reluctance to have contact with their clients. Perhaps the unwillingness to meet candidates in a competitive program is an aspect of a widespread retreat from facing difficult decisions. It is easier to deal with comparative scores on an examination, or with a dossier of written submissions, than with living, breathing, and perhaps difficult human beings. Direct encounters admittedly require rigorous assessments of character, of accomplishments, and of abilities. But that is, after all, the responsibility to be shouldered.

The selection committees are the backbone of individual support programs. If the right selectors are recruited—which takes experience and careful forethought—one can usually rest assured they will want to apply high standards, and that, rather than gimmicks, is the best assurance of fairness.

9

PUBLIC RELATIONS AND
RELATIONS WITH
THE PUBLIC

Positive public images have become increasingly important to foundations. This is not a matter of image alone; it may be a matter of the very survival of philanthropic institutions in this country. Foundations are under greater public pressure than ever before to respond to grave societal problems and to the needs in education, health, and human services caused by shutdowns in government programs. Faced with the possibility of congressional hearings that would lead to discomfiting changes, possible new taxes, and further restrictions, foundations are at a critical crossroads. Conservatives in Congress, fueled by right-wing lobbies, can intimidate foundations with threats of additional restrictions on their activities, by taxing their assets, reducing their freedom of action, and eliminating some kinds of grants, especially those that reflect a "liberal" agenda. At a time when vision and innovative leadership are sorely needed, foundations find themselves instead focused on the need for public understanding and approval of their missions more than at any other time in the history of American philanthropy. Twenty years ago, a typical foundation would ask its grantees not to publicize the source of their grant, or, if they did, to be brief and low key, and to clear the language with the foundation donor. Today, foundations have major public relations offices, sometimes called "publication offices," and trumpet the news of their funding in press releases to the media. They also hire outside publicity counsel, and every effort is made to get favorable press. They are rewarded by seeing that their grantmaking, if of general public interest, makes newsworthy copy. Unfortunately, this expert polishing of the public image is rarely accompanied by serious internal soul-searching, and where it exists, the exercise is rarely self-critical and usually serves only as a defensive measure against outside pressures and forces threatening the foundation.

Foundations have not solved the crucial problem of how the public sees them. The most obvious good relations foundations should seek and strengthen are with their natural constituencies— the individuals and institutions that are their potential or actual grantees. Ironically, it would seem that these relations are at a nadir. Though there are many reasons for this, we will see that the introduction of innovative thinking, as well as the reinstituting of some of the past practices of foundations, can have a positive effect on the situation.

Faced with a burgeoning applicant pool, unfriendly political forces, and urgent demands to alter their missions, foundations must be responsive communicators and convincing explainers of their policies and priorities. Instead, we see that foundations have responded defensively by closing off most avenues of approach and have surrounded themselves with self-serving agencies. For the average citizen, these agencies are the libraries of foundation centers in major cities, which produce source materials on foundations; the Aspen Institute–based Nonprofit Sector Research Fund, which gives grants created and funded by a group of major foundations; a host of exclusive subject-oriented "grantmakers" groups, which establish solid bulwarks of common concern and establish priorities in their fields; *Foundation News*, which is the field's semiofficial house organ; and the loosely associated Independent Sector organization. The foundations' trade association is called the Council on Foundations. All of these sources of information also try to determine the field's public image.

This bulwark against the average citizen has had its counterpart in relations with individual applicants, institutions, and potential grantees. Even making an initial approach to a foundation in hopes of getting a useful, informative response often proves to be so difficult for prospective applicants that they may give up or never even try. A simple inquiry often gets the silent treatment. It is from these experiences, all too often involving months of waiting for answers—which, if they come at all, are mostly negative and impersonal—that so many frustrated individuals and organizations conclude that you have to know somebody to get a serious hearing at a foundation. Unfortunately, more than ever before, that may be true.

As with individuals, established institutions, unless they happen to be in favor, may encounter extraordinary difficulties in getting a hearing. Inquiries and applications that are acted on are sometimes treated with a kind of haughty superiority or disdain, amounting to a grand put-down. Even successful grantees report encountering condescension and being treated as charity cases who should feel themselves lucky to be supported. One grantee seeking a renewal of support for his institution had to answer sixty separate requests for financial data. It seems that some foundations think they can get away with this less than civil behavior; their program officers think they are untouchable because no one wants to risk alienating those who they hope will one day provide the support that only foundations can give.

Before foundation officers invite an applicant into their offices, they usually ask for a letter summarizing the proposed application. What the uninitiated do not realize is that this preliminary submission gives the program administrator a hook on which to hang a declination, thereby obviating the need for an audience or a further exchange. One cannot be totally unsympathetic with today's program managers' search for a way to screen the large number of inquiries they are called upon to deal with. Perhaps some of these administrators, uncertain of their own professional qualifications, are afraid to deal with top expert talent and, given their positions, do not have to. Today, many who have been turned down feel that they have not been fairly dealt with, and this is a direct result of the perfunctory nature of the relationship. The usual explanation for a declination over the years has been that a proposal is or would be "out of program"—i.e., not among the subjects of the foundation's current field of interest. But nowadays, even where a project is squarely within published program guidelines, it is often declined with the simple explanation that nine out of ten requests are rejected (Rockefeller), or far worse odds are cited (Guggenheim).

Interestingly, only a few administrators at major foundations have explicitly said (and then only off the record) that initiatives from outside are not welcome as they used to be. But that, to a disturbing degree, is what is happening at large institutions and small, and medium-sized foundations are following suit. The executive director of one major foundation defended its new policy by saying that outside applications rarely match the foundation's programs and they therefore clutter procedures, making them expensive and inefficient. Both the director at one of the largest foundation arts program and a science officer at another foundation gave identical justification for isolationist procedures. They had both consulted "all who need to be heard" in the course of deciding on policies and programs. These are not sound arguments; they lack candor and, unfortunately, typify for the public consciousness the arrogance of administrators who increasingly make decisions without consulting knowledgeable people. These officers are developing programs and choosing applicants; yet they have inadequate knowledge of their subject matter and discipline. As John Sawyer of the Mellon Foundation made clear, too many foundation personnel think that they are hired to vent their likes and dislikes, and that foundation resources are there for them to dispose of as they see fit.

The narcissistic trend that Sawyer saw has grown in recent years. The Hitachi Foundation announced in 1995 that it would not accept unsolicited grant proposals; its own staff will henceforth initiate and determine where grants will go. In an inadvertent caricature of the entire scene, Hitachi's president explained: "We are being unfair to accept proposals when such a small percentage could succeed!" Rick MacArthur, president of the J. Roderick MacArthur Foundation, let it be known that "Future grant applications will not be accepted and cannot be returned. . . . Grants will be made at the sole discretion of the Board. No staff will be available either to communicate with potential donees or discuss potential grants . . . no Foundation staff member will be available to discuss this change in policy." Such attitudes undermine the integrity of the entire field of private foundations and erode the public support foundations might rally if another hostile congressional investigation takes place.

Few foundations have given explanations for turning away the applicant stream or are even prepared to say publicly that that is what they are doing. The only explanations that have come from the likes of Hitachi and J. R. MacArthur is that it saves money on staff. If saving money is their objective, then why do they not give away the assets and close their doors for good? A plausible argument can be made for foundations to hire *more* staff, because good support staff can make a program administrator more productive and a foundation more cost-effective.

A positive relationship for foundations in the past was the ongoing professional involvement a junior fellow had with a foundation officer who was conversant with the recipient's subject and could communicate with him on that level. Such relationships were not markedly different from those at universities between senior and younger scholars or in professional circles, such as between partners and law associates. A good foundation officer kept up with the progress of his grantees, showed interest, and found other ways of helping than by funding—for example, by facilitating introductions to scholars or editors, to libraries, or to public officials in this country and abroad. Significant ongoing relationships started this way, benefiting award recipients as well as the sponsoring foundations by furthering communication between their officers and creative individuals in the field. The psychological gap that exists now between scholars and artists and their foundations is due in large part to the fact that support today is given for a specific project rather than for career development or exploration of frontiers of a discipline, and projects do not last long.

In the MacArthur Foundation's first years and with the Whiting Foundation's Writers Awards, and with a few others, the procedures are different, and so, too, is the relationship between grantees and foundation officers. These are more ambitious programs, in which recognition and support are given in more ways than just with a grant or a fellowship. Such support, however, must always be offered sensitively. For example, two MacArthur Prize Fellow designees in the very first year asked the foundation not to publicize their awards. They feared the banalities of notoriety that would greet the announcement, as if they were lottery winners. Rod MacArthur reacted as if they were ungrateful and refused their request; the foundation, he said, insisted on publicity. Other MacArthur fellows asked to postpone starting their award for a year, to be better prepared to make use of it. This request, too, was rejected. Both decisions served the convenience and ego of the foundation rather than the needs of its grantees.

Some Prize Fellows enjoyed the public attention from the award, while others were nearly overwhelmed by the pressure. This explains why two MacArthur nominees who learned of their candidacy in the early years of the program asked not to be considered. They feared the distraction from their work more than they valued the potential of being recipients. For similar reasons, there have been reluctant candidates for the three-year Lila Wallace writers' awards. An inflexible requirement is that recipients affiliate themselves with an organization, institution, or program to which they give services during their award years. The condition was imposed by Lila Wallace's board chair, who let it be known that if writers are to get financial awards, they should "give something back to society." As if writers and other artists, by doing their work, are not contributing to society at all times!

The public image of foundations is also determined by their principal programs and achievements. For example, after the Second World War, foundations made energetic efforts to rebuild intellectual capital and institutions in Europe. Later, the Ford and Rockefeller Foundations undertook major development efforts in Asia, Africa, and Latin America. Parallel initiatives in the United States created area studies programs at universities and at research institutes focused on single countries or areas of the world where in the last ten years foundation leaders have rediscovered international responsibilities and new opportunities. Currently in vogue are studies of "the global biosphere," energy policy, international community development, the creation of philanthropic capital in developing countries.

But enthusiasms come and go in foundations, and looking at past patterns, one may well ask what is around the next corner. The willingness to reconsider policies and objectives is a strength of private foundations, but sometimes, especially recently, successful programs have been dropped for unexplained reasons, without historic insight or future perspective, it seems. A major example of this is the Rockefeller Foundation's international fellowship program; another is the Ford Foundation's performing arts program.

In most foundations, informal approaches for support have given way to highly structured procedures, which have affected relations with the public. Informal discussions made for easier relations and better mutual understanding. Today's formal applications can be so onerous as to turn off all but those institutions with fully staffed development offices. Information in excruciating detail may be required. Institutions and individuals permitted to apply report that the waiting time before there is any kind of result gets longer and longer. Proposals must pass through more offices than ever before. Some foundations have set up internal committees and formalized procedures that rival government bureaucracies. Applicants invited for discussions of their proposals may experience confrontation—perhaps not intentional—which is emblematic of a fundamental change from a time when foundation officers had collegial relationships with fellow professionals. There was no "we/thee" posture. "But that is no longer so important," one young administrator said, "because our programs now are proactive."

Public relations in a time of politically correct influences on programs, ostensibly aimed at those most deserving based on quality, has created special problems for foundations. For example, a new requirement initiated by the Ford Foundation, which is being copied elsewhere, is a prime example of Robert Brustein's "coercive philanthropy": full disclosure of the racial composition of the applying institution's board. With political correctness a condition, a prospective applicant can be eliminated on that ground alone, giving credence to suspicions that "winners" are predetermined. Foundations have brought these suspicions on themselves, as so many of their activities appear to be affected by prevailing politically correct considerations. Not long ago, at one of the largest foundations, the creator of a new program was told by a senior official to appoint a selection committee consisting of a majority of minority representatives. Even the suspicion that a foundation activity is being perverted in this way—regardless of the motivation—inhibits free-flowing intercourse with outside scholars, officials, and artists, and casts doubt on a program's integrity.

It is simply not appropriate to dilute the goal of recognizing the most talented individuals by giving a percentage of awards to specific groups. That may serve a public relations purpose, but if such programs cannot put quality ahead of all other considerations, foundations should not be carrying them on at all. There is, of course, a further danger: as political correctness is rolled back, it would be tragic if there was to be a backlash preventing aboveboard compensatory activities specifically for designated minorities.

10

AFTER THE CHECK IS IN THE MAIL: MONITORING AND EVALUATION

Foundations tend not to be introspective. They often discuss "vision," but their business is pragmatism. Their bottom line is the amount of money spent on what they decide is worthy of support. Foundations all try to distinguish their activities from others', and most are really not interested in critically evaluating the results of their handiwork by comparing what was accomplished to what might have been accomplished or to what the aspirations for their programs might have been. Largely, they are beholden unto themselves.

In order to improve internal workings as well as strengthen external impact—the public face of their efforts—some foundations in recent years decided they would examine their performance, focusing particularly on the means they use and the ends they seek. In essence, these inquiries raised issues of quality and efficacy: Is this indeed an activity that achieves the desired goal, as we have defined it, and as we have, following that definition, sought to achieve it? Is this producing what we expected? If not, are we even focusing on the right issues? Or should we, in fact, be doing something completely different? These evaluations have not come easily. A few foundations have gone so far as to create internal evaluation offices.

When he retired in 1971 as chairman of the board of the Rockefeller Foundation, John D. Rockefeller III commented:

> *I cannot emphasize too strongly the need for constant critical review of programs and a continuing willingness to reexamine established assumptions. In my opinion, terminating programs that have, so to speak, completed their missions is often as difficult—and necessary—as the wise selection of new programs. In both cases, flexibility as to change is the basic requirement.*

Foundation officials too often look upon evaluation as a way to count scores rather than as a significant source of learning about the subject of a grant and about how one accomplishes certain purposes. Evaluation is a form of competition. Did we get noticed? Did we do better than other of the foundation's programs? Did we do better than rival foundations? How many awards have we won in this program? How many grantees have published books and how many books have they published? Often, what is weighed is more quantitative, oriented toward some dimly perceived "bottom line," than qualitative.

Moreover, evaluation—so difficult in the fields of science, art, and scholarship—has special difficulty in the foundation world, inasmuch as everyone involved is usually terribly sensitive to the outcome. Self-evaluation by a foundation's staff is an especially tricky exercise, because people who are themselves responsible for putting a program together and for operating it are bound to be somewhat defensive about its success or lack of success. But are outside consultants better? Who is truly "outside" in the sense of disinterested? In many cases, outside consultants could be actual or potential grantees—harboring the hope that the foundation might be interested in what an individual scholar, a department, an institution, an orchestra, is doing—and would thus be reluctant to bite the hand that someday might feed them. Foundations sometimes employ relatively inexperienced consultants who are without independent standing, who are in it for the money. It is difficult to understand why foundations enlist such people when senior professional consultants are as willing today to do this as they were thirty to forty years ago—unless foundations are worried about what they would conclude.

Elizabeth McCormack, who has many years of foundation experience and is chair of the MacArthur Foundation's board, addressed these issues in a speech a few years ago. She espoused a system of objective evaluation created by the community of foundations:

> *Other institutions in the non-profit sector are made accountable. If an educational institution is inadequate, it will, in the long run, cease to attract students. If the artistic performance of an arts organization is mediocre, sooner or later people will stop coming to see the ballet or listen to the music. In a foundation, it is not so. People will hesitate to criticize us because they fear the criticism will keep us from making appropriate grants. Therefore, we must evaluate ourselves.*

But she warned: "Self-evaluation is difficult. Self-deception is easy." Indeed.

McCormack suggested a structural way to make use first of self-evaluation and then of outside consultation:

> *I suggest outside evaluation would profit foundations immeasurably. Educational institutions are evaluated voluntarily by their peers. I suggest such an evaluation*

would be most appropriate for foundations. Wouldn't it be wise for the Council on Foundations to create an evaluation arm to which foundations could apply for criticism? Teams of peers would then visit a foundation, having received a self-evaluation report. Self-evaluation would be, I suggest, more honest if it were to be read, reviewed, studied by peers, who would then visit the foundation to determine whether or not its assessment of itself is adequate.

The problem with this suggestion is that McCormack has based her recommendation for the use of peer review on what is the accepted and generally effective system of evaluation of schools and colleges in the United States. But in the foundation world, because of the money at stake, outsiders may in fact be interested parties, who will hesitate to criticize foundations for fear of repercussions. Why would an assessment arm of an industry group like the Council on Foundations be any more candid? Professional guilds have a propensity to protect their members. Still, McCormack's suggestions are steps toward a solution that deserve serious consideration; they are likely to lead to more useful results than either of the alternatives alone: self-evaluation or the use of mercenary consultants.

For any sort of evaluation, of course, one has to know the objectives of the activity being examined. One should also know the purpose of evaluation. Is it to strengthen the program? To replace it? What do the board and the administration of the institution have in mind? Are the results being judged, or is one trying to judge the process leading to the results? Is one comparing the program under scrutiny to other projects by the same foundation or to those by other foundations? Is one aim of the evaluation to gauge the adequacy of the staff of the program? Is the purpose to assess the publicity the program has generated for a cause that the foundation has in mind—in the health field, for example, or in agriculture? Or is the evaluation merely a routine exercise, enacted complacently and without a serious purpose?

If the activity under review is a program that supports individuals, then there are quite specific and differentiated questions one might ask, especially if a purpose of the assessment is to measure the impact the project has had on individual activity, progress, growth, and achievement. An essential question is whether the program has in fact facilitated the work of the individual whom the foundation wanted to aid. Does the program add credibility—to a person or to an idea—that was absent before the directed effort took place? Then, of course, one also looks at the particular selection process employed, comparing it to procedures in similar programs. One also, in the end, wants to know whether the long-term results of support for an individual contributed to knowledge, or art, or whether there was some other kind of contribution, such as the intellectual development of the individual, or no discernible contribution at all. The nature of the contribution is most difficult to establish; who knows what could have been accomplished without foundation support? Certainly foundations should not be too quick to take credit.

The timing of an evaluation is important. Some foundation observers advocate bringing outside consultants in at the inception of the planning process for a particular program. The evaluators monitoring the activity (foundations and grantors permitting) can thereby get in on the ground floor and know from listening, if not participating, what the objectives of the activity are from the start. Evaluators can thus understand how the program's objectives were defined, how decisions were made about procedures, how staffing was determined, what obstacles were encountered, and so forth. The evaluation process requires total immersion, foresight, prudent judgment, patience. The potential benefits for everyone involved in the foundation's mission are worth the effort.

The typical foundation program evaluation, however, has a consultant taking a look at a project that began without his or her involvement a year to five years earlier. The "expert," coming from the outside, is expected to "poke around" and then offer universal pearls of wisdom about what the program has or has not achieved. This inspector-general approach is obviously very different from that of an evaluator who was "present at the creation"; it leads to a completely different kind of result, sometimes useless except for the ego gratification of having had an "expert" say, "You are doing just fine."

More candor is possible with an evaluator who is involved from the beginning as the "friend of the court," as it were, because he or she knows exactly what the foundation is trying to achieve. The foundation's staff and the evaluator can grow comfortable with one another and exchange ideas throughout the program's evolution. There is opportunity for intimate back-and-forth discussion for genuine exchange, and the result is not simply one individual's view of a program at some remove from it and after the fact. This lessens the burden on the evaluator, and he or she becomes part adviser, part reviewer. It makes the review a vital part of the program.

Whichever system of evaluation is chosen, the spirit in which the assessment is conducted matters tremendously. Foundations must use evaluators of strong character, extensive experience, and unquestioned maturity. Neither timidity nor aggressiveness is appropriate in this role. An evaluator must possess intelligence and insight. He or she must not confuse the search for validity with a search for absolute certainty and must accept the usefulness of a foundation's failures. Evaluation is for people who appreciate the virtues of anomaly, ambivalence, and even paradox. The best attitude with which the whole enterprise is undertaken is one of giving rather than judging, of recognizing the importance of helping grantees and fellows to be more creative than they are. In short, the role of those who are official critics of foundation activity is one that should not be left to egotists or second-rate minds.

One example of a successful "present at the creation" evaluation can be found in the early years of the MacArthur Prize Fellowship Program. With the board's approval, President John Corbally acted on the staff's recommendation to invite F. Champion Ward, a distinguished member of the foundation world, to be a consultant throughout the course of the program as it was put together and implemented.

Ward had full access to the office, to files, and to every discussion. He was privy to all research. He was on the premises frequently, and participated, at least as an observer, in staff meetings. He attended the meetings of the selection committee and the board so that he could track the process all the way from the initial nomination of an individual right through board action.

This dynamic process proved tremendously valuable because the staff was able to have a constant flow of information about the inventive new program and could fashion its procedures as the program evolved. Everybody benefited: the selection committee, the staff of the program, members of the board, even the future grantees. All gained insight from Ward's broad experience and sharp eye on what was going on from a point of view unavailable to those who were full-time insiders. For example, we had decided that we would not bother recipients with detailed questions and intrusive labors of any kind that we felt would be contrary to both the spirit and the letter of the Prize Fellowships. But Ward made the argument that we might lose the insights into what happened at the very beginning of this program—particularly the award's impact on recipients—if we did not solicit their views. Thus Ward gently interviewed the initial group of Prize Fellow recipients within a year of their obtaining the award.

Another interesting example of a useful evaluation process comes from the Bush Foundation in Minneapolis–Saint Paul, known for its high-quality programs in the arts in Minnesota and the region. The foundation's officers obviously took the mandate for a critique seriously; their concern is evident from the ambitious questions asked and answered, including: What is the program accomplishing? What is its impact on the fellows who receive support, on other artists, on the arts community of Minnesota, on the cultural life of Minnesota?

The Bush Foundation's staff instructed the evaluators to assess how the fellowships enhanced or hindered the quality of learning—as distinguished from the career development—of their recipients and whether the fellowship advanced or changed previous directions of work. They also asked for an assessment of the awards' impact during the grant period and for periods beyond the termination of the fellowships. The evaluators examined the liabilities, drawbacks, or other negative aspects of the fellowships. The foundation was interested in the views of all participants, instructing the evaluators to interview not just the artists selected for support but those candidates who were not chosen. The Bush Foundation wanted a full appraisal, warts and all. The results were textured and informative and led to beneficial, important program changes.

Another interesting case, though one having a more contentious outcome, was the stem-to-stern assessment of the Ford Foundation's management by Merrimon Cuninggim in the 1970s. Cuninggim, who had been president of the Danforth Foundation for many years, was known within the community as a thoughtful and insightful senior foundation leader. McGeorge Bundy, president of Ford at the time, invited Cuninggim into the foundation for the purpose of poking around and doing whatever it was that he might wish to do to be able to advise the president and senior staff as to how well they were doing.

Cuninggim's title was Adviser on Program Management; he was given the run of the whole foundation and of its files and per-

sonnel. Joined by a former colleague from the Danforth Foundation, Cuninggim traveled around the country and abroad to look
into nearly everything that touched on Ford's management. It ap-
peared that Ford was saying to him, Come on in; we know you
are not going to feel pressure here to make your conclusions fit
any preconceptions; there is nothing that goes on here that we
want to hide from you; we would really like to know in all candor
what you would propose.

Before he was through, Cuninggim submitted ten or a dozen
major reports to Bundy and the board and over forty memoranda
on minor matters. He was frank and critical about Ford's business, particularly how it decided upon candidates for specific individual grants. The result was so much consternation among
precisely the people who had invited him that his tenure was
shortened (although he left on the best of personal terms with
Bundy and other senior officers). Indeed, the first sentence of
Cuninggim's subsequent report and analysis virtually tells the
whole story: "Once upon a time I had a job that nobody else had
ever had before, nor is it ever likely to be repeated." This is eloquent evidence that program evaluations are sensitive data. Foundations do not make them public, and if they compare notes with
one another, they do so *entre nous.* Evaluation information, especially when critical, is rarely shared, even among officers within a
foundation, which unfortunately reduces the usefulness of the
information.

Why was the Bush Foundation open to a report that mixed
praise and criticism, whereas the Ford Foundation flew into an institutional huff at the suggestion that all was not perfect in the
realm? The answer has to do with the way different foundations
regard their roles. Those that see their mission as one of risking
and experimenting, of inaugurating bold new programs, of trying
things out and falling short and learning by doing, will usually
treat evaluation of their work as an essential part of their explo-

ration and will not worry about the negatives that might evolve from such monitoring. They expect criticism and clear-eyed assessments of program "duds"; they do not expect all of their programs to succeed, except on relatively few occasions. That is the nature of the activity; it is very much what the scientist does in the laboratory when he or she will pose a hypothesis and then, based upon that, do work that either will or will not have the desired result. Even if it does not, one has not only learned something but in fact achieved something.

Most foundations have a simpler view of themselves, however. Their institutional goal is to push grant money out the door, not take creative risks. Money going out the door is intended to produce expected results and certainly not to embarrass the foundation by falling short of the objectives. In this way the staff gets satisfaction from the board's approval, the foundation's image remains sunny, and no one sticks out in any unconventional manner. The very things, therefore, that the Bush Foundation's staff strove to understand—how well or poorly they were doing their job, what other approaches they might try to improve programs— are actually the last things many foundation officers want to know. This puts the foundation profession in the position of the aircraft industry, ordering design changes only after enough cracks have become blatantly visible, or worse.

Convincing accountability across the board for foundations is long overdue, and serious evaluations taken seriously are essential to their missions. Critical understanding provides a self-reflective way of pursuing a foundation's responsibilities. Having found out as much as one can about the strengths and weaknesses of a foundation's performance, one can improve the odds that more of the foundation's money will be spent boldly. And creatively.

11

ROOM FOR IMPROVEMENT

We need foundations that are user-friendly, with policies that emanate from the society of scholars and practitioners, not ones imposed on them. We need foundation officers who see themselves as part of a spectrum of colleagues prepared to listen and engage in open discussion, not as an aloof class who exercise their authority and disdain discussion. This calls for significant changes.

A principal theme of the preceding chapters has been the important role of foundations in identifying the most talented individuals of every age in order to support their creativity. That responsibility is not an abstraction; it follows from society's greatest needs and asks more foundations to do what some have done so well in the past. There is need for leadership in all our most important fields of endeavor, from pure scholarly inquiry to problem solving, defining critical issues, giving the electorate a chance to understand these issues and their urgency, and creating public direction in social, educational, and political arenas.

McNeil Lowry put it this way:

We have to find and support the oddball creative fanat-ics. No one is doing that. Philanthropy is afraid of criti-cism, and there are many opportunists using the arts as scapegoats. There are always artists out there making the sacrifice to perfect their work. There have to be long-term serious commitments made. In a way we are back to where we were in the 1950s when I first started tapping into philanthropy in a big way. I'd go for the risks now like we did then and go on risking all the time.

Lowry's focus was on the arts, but his meaning is clear for other subjects and purposes.

The urgent need for new leadership results from the virtual abdication of responsibility by the senior intellectual elite and their dwindling numbers in the academies, political life, and else-where in society. It is only in the economy that we find an identi-fiable group in control, in such a concentration of power that they are our most evident elite. This reflects one of our deep-seated problems in the United States: the widening gulf between poverty and wealth, which is morally reprehensible and politically explo-sive. "There is nothing more dangerous," said Dr. Martin Luther King, Jr., "than to build a society with a large segment of people in that society who feel they have no stake in it." The rich are getting richer, the poor are getting poorer, and the middle class has to run just as fast as it can to stay in the same place. The poor are our fastest-growing discriminated-against minority.

A nation cannot live at peace when the gap between affluence and poverty, which also means between the powerful and the im-potent, continues to widen. The elite of the economy, those who manipulate the country's financial and industrial capacities, have to a devastating degree abandoned responsibility for the commu-nities that business exists to serve. We need leadership to fill this vacuum, leadership with fidelity to the public interest. Foundations, because they exercise different priorities than Wall Street, are in a position to catalyze that change. They have the intellectual leverage and sufficient funding to make a difference. They are uniquely placed to make the kind of investments that will enlarge the pool of human capital from which we can draw leadership in strategic sectors of society. Foundations are not (or should not be) subject to political agendas. Therefore, they can take the lead on questions that have become politically untouchable; being independent, they can take on projects that have fallen out of fashion or favor and, taking the long view, stick with them. Although foundations control only a tiny percentage of the gross national product, they are disproportionately capable of defining and working on the most daunting of our society's deficits. Foundations can identify and unleash talent that is currently untapped or unrecognized as well as potential major players who need to be recruited and given opportunities to develop their abilities and focus them.

The nation's cultural and political elite, in other words, need to be augmented and empowered. The reality is that what Christopher Lasch calls "the cultural elite" have "lost faith in the values, or what remains of them, of the West." Most are out of the mainstream, carrying on sidebar discussions with one another. Their intellectual vitality has been sapped, flaring up in the marketplace only when their education and convictions are challenged, as by the cultural separatists.

Today, when we need compassionate moral and political leadership, there is indifference—born of cynicism, despair, or in some circles, of intolerance or greed—to the suffering of the homeless, the needs of the rootless young, the infirm, the weak. This neglectful attitude is best exemplified by the righteously indignant Gingrich House of Representatives. Such callousness has been growing since the Lyndon Johnson administration.

Philanthropic venture capital alone cannot turn our institutions and political practices around, but it is the best means we have to identify and support gifted individuals for the immense job. That, along with carefully prepared, long-term support of our cultural and scientific institutions, stands a chance of galvanizing government at all levels to give the prudent leadership required of it.

What are some of the major problems to which foundations—and the talents they can unleash—should pay greatest attention?

Processes of societal deterioration and near moral collapse have progressed at accelerating rates; this deterioration has been far more pronounced than is generally realized by the average citizen. The fear of violence, especially of crime, is omnipresent. Particularly where children are concerned, it is our most urgent priority to bring this epidemic under control, and we need new thinking and new approaches for this task.

For example, in 1993, according to the Center to Prevent Handgun Violence, every day up to 65 American men, women, and children were killed with handguns. In 1990, the figure for the entire year for Sweden was 13; for Switzerland, 91; for Canada, 68; for Great Britain, 22; for the United States, 10,567. With millions now buying semiautomatic weapons and a new generation of young men on the streets, the death rate is going up.

How we treat our children tests who we are. Marian Wright Edelman, president of the Children's Defense Fund, says a child is reported abused or neglected every thirteen seconds. Substance abuse increases daily. Our prisons are bulging; the recidivist rate proves the prison experience is not a deterrent. Is anything of relevance to our problem to be learned from the Netherlands, where hashish and some other drugs have been legalized and are freely available and where there is the lowest imprisonment rate in the world? Violence today is unparalleled in our violence-prone history; a part of the population has lost self-control; another significant fraction has stopped caring except for its own hide. Is it not time for a newly underwritten investigation, by fresh, caring minds, into the nature and possible control of the violence epidemic? Is this not the province of the foundation?

There are other pressing issues. The Carnegie-sponsored Flexner Report of 1910 and the follow-up by Rockefeller's General Education Board led to the reform of medical education and the strengthening of that entire profession. Today, the legal profession has invaded every aspect of our personal and professional lives, and it is hard not to see the destructive effect on the fabric of our lives. Why has not some foundation enlisted the talent it takes to do for the legal profession what the Flexner Report eighty-five years ago spurred for the medical profession?

To relieve the pressure of the ghettos, a network of boarding schools for black youngsters has been created in recent years. African-American educators, including superintendents of major urban school systems with high black crime rates, and the parents of school-age youngsters, want to create more such boarding schools. Carrying out this plan will take new funding, in which foundations will be called upon to participate. But they can also play an important brokering role, by creating a network of experts who will help create, staff, and direct the new schools.

When the dust settles on the twentieth century, a diversified, pluralistic culture rather than a series of separate cultures making up a multicultural mélange will predominate. Unfortunately, most foundations will not have contributed toward that end, having chosen instead to support separatists and multiculturalists. Perhaps this has grown out of a confusion of guilt feelings and responses to the genuine need of black and other minority Americans who sought help in retrieving the particular experience of their heritage. The long, loud exaggerated struggle over multiculturalism has obscured many real ills, especially among the young. Worrying about the education of the young is an old man's disease, Socrates said. We have seen how little this country invests in its children, and we are paying the price for it. Young people of school and university age, regardless of race, suffer from the complementary diseases of self-absorption and fascination with violence. Brutalizing, desensitizing media violence is a fitting accomplice to their introversion, as is the influence of the narcissism that dominates so many in the generation of their parents. Some people believe that sweeping change will come about only with a reversal in the neglect of our principal public institutions. Even then, a change in the attitude of youth is not going to take place without leadership. Right now one is hard-pressed to know where that will come from.

There is hardly a "domestic" issue foundations can work on that does not have international repercussions. Primary among them is population control. According to the World Bank, 700 million of the world's 5.6 billion people now face endemic hunger, and the expectation is that the world's population will grow by at least 2 billion in the next two decades. The transforming technology, which can bring about large increases in food production, cannot keep pace. The International Rice Research Institute in the Philippines, created by Rockefeller and Ford Foundations, recently developed a type of rice that would increase harvests 20 to 25 percent, but at about the same time this was announced, the Worldwatch Institute estimated that the demand for rice in Asia in the next thirty-five years will double as the population soars.

One of the most portentous issues of our time is the spread of nuclear and biological weapons and their delivery systems. A few foundations have ongoing studies about control of weapons of mass destruction, but many more resources need to be devoted to this subject.

Regrettably, foundations rarely find a genuine moral reference point for important new ventures and for making difficult choices. On the subjects of human gene research, we cannot afford to fail to find such a stance. The profound ethical, legal, environmental, and innumerable other implications of using the powers made possible by gene identification and therapy and the possibility of predetermining characteristics need every bit of the attention the best-qualified minds can give. Hypotheses based on evidence of a genetic basis for some criminal and aggressive behavior, for example, are now rapidly being worked on; the lid is off many prior restrictions on human genetic therapy. The beneficial potential is great; the hazards are probably greater. The subject requires a concentration of the keenest scientific minds, but just as important are those others who can best comprehend the necessity and means of controlling these emerging powers.

The potential disasters around us—poverty, disease, violence, child deprivation and abuse, impingement on women's rights, decay of infrastructures, environmental degradation, deterioration of public services, ideological extremism—have a common denominator: the loss of our shared values. McNeil Lowry observed that among public policy issues and questions, one is too often overlooked, and it is basic: "the recognition of a value system in which humanism, humaneness, a sense of personal identity and creativity liberate personal and moral faculties." In allocating resources for building and nourishing future leadership, the priority should be given to where we are too often penurious and neglectful—to the sources of ideas, values, beliefs, convictions—the humanities and arts. Several deep prejudices need to be overcome. One of them is that only the sciences, or, conceivably, the "practical" social sciences, point most directly to solutions for us. Another is that religions are the only meaningful source of lasting values. Morals and ethics continue to be closely identified in the public mind with organized religion. But most organized religion in the United States is not intellectually oriented. It does not ask questions; it only has answers. Americans still have a propensity to mistrust a historian or philosopher, a poet or dramatist, who has a vision and an imagination, but these same people may follow in droves the spellbinding TV visionaries who claim to have a monopoly on truth.

Thirty years ago, the biologist Robert Morison wrote: "It is in their support of the humanities that the major foundations are most frequently criticized. They are said to be both timid and inept. Above all, they fail to understand the importance of individual effort and achievement and to find appropriate ways of supporting it." This has not changed, unfortunately. Although scientists such as Morison are not in doubt that humanists have something important to say about such issues as the use of nuclear power, uncontrolled population growth, genetic engineering, there are others who remain unpersuaded.

The essence of the humanities is the provision for making informed choices. Today, those choices rarely have universal appeal; the intellectual and moral values that underlie both the arts and the humanities are, of course, controversial. They disturb some and anger others. They are more apt to clarify differences than to promote agreement, but they can lead to consensus on free inquiry and nonviolent acceptance of differences. In our schools and universities and beyond, the study of man's moral relations with others is surely no less important than it was; it is also a keynote of the treatment of minority races by the majority and, increasingly, vice versa.

If what humanists have to contribute to society's leadership as well as its formative development is important, then they deserve a higher priority in foundation plans than they received hitherto. The NEH's existence cannot be counted on, given that its sparse constituency is difficult to organize in the face of its despoilers; and government should not predominate in support of the humanities in any event. These missions of supporting individuals and giving the humanities priority not only are reconcilable but are indissolubly linked. McNeil Lowry made the case this way:

> *If we think only collectively, we do not really penetrate the darkness. It is only when we think of individuals that we dare again to bet on humanity, on humanism, on the humanizing and civilizing forces in art, philosophy, music, literature and language. However unprovable, even untenable, the wager may be, it has the virtue of necessity. We need it to go on. Without it, there is only solipsism, nihilism and despair.*

An example of an imaginative, pacesetting initiative toward "penetrating the darkness" was the Ford Foundation's 1967–1975 fellowship-program initiative in rural America. The Leadership Development Program differed from other fellowship efforts in that the seven hundred people selected for it were not chosen for their academic qualifications and were not enrolled in programs of academic study or research. Men and women were selected primarily because they had demonstrated a capacity for personal initiative regarding the problems in their communities. They had few traditional credentials. They were young, and all of them were interested in doing something about the difficulties that poverty and race present for people in getting ahead. Each of these fellows had an individually tailored program that exposed him or her to extensive travel, new experiences, personal stresses, and some rethinking of careers. It amounted to the invention of a radical new form of fellowship. The experimental nature of the program, its insistence on empiricism, its refusal to establish simple criteria for selecting fellows, resulted in seven hundred individually tailored programs.

Taking people who would otherwise never have been touched, the program operated on an unprovable but exciting proposition: If you provide individuals with new tools and skills, real work will be done and changes for the better will occur. The application of rigid rules to any part of this program would soon have destroyed its originality. Recruiting for it was difficult and depended increasingly on word-of-mouth contacts and on fellows themselves urging likely candidates to apply.

For exciting initiatives such as this, foundations can establish a cadre of scouts, roving spotters of talent, who travel around and poke about, spending time at local colleges, science labs, regional theaters, community organizations, and other enterprises—and then report to the foundation. This can work very effectively if, say, the MacArthur Foundation wants to give awards or enlist creative people from all walks of life, including the academies, though not only in the usual disciplines. If, in other words, one's goal is to ferret out precisely those people who are ignored by others—the ones who function across the lines of disciplines and professions, often unacknowledged by the several that they bridge—then one is likely to find that kind of person through scouts who have the time and the ability to do their looking patiently in a great variety of communities. It would make sense to set some of them loose on a given piece of turf, saying, for example, "For the next year, North and South Dakota are your beat. This is how much we are paying you, and we will also pay for food, lodging, and travel. You can journey wherever you wish within those two states. We want to hear from you about people who you think are worthy of consideration as candidates for our program."

Another approach—discipline-based—is for a foundation to recruit an expert in American history, say, asserting, "We will pay you a year's salary, and we will pay for your meals, hotels, and transportation. You can go wherever you want in the United States or, conceivably, even abroad, to find exceptionally talented young people working in the area of American history." It would be a commission, a hunting license for talent in a specific field. This scout would obviously focus more narrowly than the person assigned to turf such as North and South Dakota. But either way, through the use of such extended eyes and ears, there is a good chance of finding what one would not otherwise find.

Other new approaches that foundations might consider primarily involve comparing notes with others, pooling experience, sharing information. Those responsible for programs that support talented individuals should be talking to one another more. Except for the sciences, they know remarkably little about what their colleagues are doing, even in the same fields. Foundations compete far more than they cooperate. They tend to be secretive. This is not true across the board: foundation officers in medical research or in the environmental areas know what others are doing. Why is there such ignorance and secretiveness, so many jealousies, such competitiveness, among individual grant programs in most other fields and disciplines? This is narcissism, and it has no rational place in the foundation world.

A very few nonscience foundations have made admirable efforts to share their experience with other philanthropies. The Bush Foundation and the Jerome Foundation, both with offices in Minneapolis, have made serious and unique efforts to clue in their colleagues as to what they are doing and even to give them a free run of evaluations that have been made of their activities. Margaret Mahoney, president emeritus of the Commonwealth Fund, counsels foundations sensibly to learn from one another what does and does not work, to share knowledge about talent, and to invite participation in the development of new projects. Not many take this constructive approach to heart.

One innovative idea for sharing information would benefit both foundations and potential grantees: the establishment of a clearinghouse of dossiers for interested, eligible, and competitive candidates. Hundreds of individuals are nominated or submit applications to private and public foundations, looking for a piece of the philanthropic pie. Much knowledge is acquired about a great many people in myriad fields, who have done solid work and are now ready to do more. But sponsoring agencies can select and support only a small number, rejecting most candidates, including some who are highly qualified.

Now, in most cases, very few of those who present themselves are serious candidates for the exceptional kind of support being offered. But there are in fact many more highly talented people who come to the attention of foundation programs than there are funds available at any one time. What happens, typically, is that after the selections are made, those who were fully considered but not chosen get sent out into orbit with a rejection letter, as it were, perhaps never to be heard from again. Their information is filed or discarded.

Yet there is a way of preserving rather than wasting this resource. Foundation officers could be asked to present the names of individuals who have come to their attention but who have, by some issue other than their high quality, failed to receive support. These select candidates with excellent qualifications could be organized and cross-indexed by subject, discipline, region, and other categories, information that could be made available to other foundations, organizations, or individuals interested in considering them for support. These interested grant givers would include wealthy professionals who seek to "give something back," companies and other professional groups who have charitable-giving programs, and small family foundations.

An example will reveal the simplicity and usefulness of this idea. Suppose a foundation is considering nonfiction writers, and fifteen are invited to apply. Further suppose that the foundation decides to give fellowships to five of them. Among the remaining ten, there may well be two or three writers of high quality who might have received fellowships if the foundation's budget had stretched farther or if their particular projects had been more attuned to the foundation's mission. Instead of being lost in the process, they might qualify for support from another source. With these writers' permission, and with the help of a clearinghouse that receives data about them, the writers' needs could be brought to the attention of other grantmaking individuals or agencies, possibly smaller ones, in other parts of the country, that do not have the staff needed to assemble expert panels and publicize their agenda, but are nevertheless interested in supporting writers.

Critical to the success of this idea is that none of the recycled applicants be perceived as "rejects." It is true that the remaining two or three writers were not in the original foundation's top five, but they might have been selected if the foundation's budget had been larger. Thus it was not their lack of talent but the foundation's limited resources or program that determined the outcome.

One obstacle to this venture is, of course, that same reluctance of foundation officers to share information and to offer applicants' names and attributes to such a pool. The tendency, strongest in the most narcissistic institutions, is to believe that their program is unique; they do not want to play at all with other institutions. But if a clearinghouse existed, there would undoubtedly be foundation officers who would see that they were saying a final, definitive "no" to fewer people or, at least, would be giving a second chance to many applicants as a result of a clearinghouse's outreach. Some foundation people would be pleased by this and abandon their habits of territoriality and exclusivity. No formal mechanism to share information about talented individuals has ever existed. But to serve the best interests of scholars, artists, scientists, activists, and others who rely on philanthropic support, foundations can perhaps rally behind such a potentially helpful innovation.

Foundations need to make a credo of risk taking; they also need to follow through. It is not uncommon for a philanthropy to give vigorous lip service to this notion and then to follow up with little or no truly bold actions. Foundation watcher Waldemar Nielsen, as noted, has been blunt on this point. Foundations' "vaunted" theory, "endlessly repeated," that they are "innovative, pro-active, targeted and strategic" have not helped the nation find solutions to its principal problems. "Are these merely hopes and intentions?" asks Nielsen. On the other hand, there is hopeful evidence that some foundations do have the vision to give grants to some extraordinary nonprofit organizations, like the Children's Defense Fund, that may have exceptionally talented, courageous leadership, such as the CDF's Marian Edelman.

Foundations are in the judgment business; they have to choose—an important mission is to distinguish between extraordinary individuals and merely good ones—and not take on all comers. Foundation missions are betrayed when they make a foolish virtue of egalitarianism and a useless myth of excellence. They end up sacrificing quality for access. Often, this results from a confusion in the program's guiding vision, which in turn stems from failure to think through its objectives at the outset, or to have them at all.

Selection criteria and procedures need to be specifically formulated for each activity. Frequently, foundations clone from other programs methods of identifying candidates, ending up with procedures that are not appropriate for the purpose of their own program. Moreover, foundation staffs need to create and fine-tune procedures and operate them themselves. Hiring outside consultants to administer their programs is costly and inappropriate. Profit-making consultants are apt to invent procedural shortcuts and politically correct formulas in efforts to please their foundation clients. These deviate from a noble purpose, and if foundation programs cannot put quality before all other consideration, they should not be carried on at all.

To this end, program officers assigned to direct organized individual grant programs need to be the best a foundation can attract. The activity demands a fair amount of experience and sophistication to enlist first-rate selectors who meet the test of top-flight creativity and intellectual rigor.

Foundations need a broader conception of their role. Supporting individual grantees involves more than simply paying out an award. That role begins with the all-important factor of timing of the award, which should meet the recipient's needs, preference, and convenience. The foundation's support should emphasize giving recognition (at the time of the award), ongoing encouragement, help with whatever the work requires, such as introductions—all without intruding or imposing. Such nurturing support is often useful beyond the formal terms of the award. To style and administer these awards simply as "a grant" of money, as so often happens, is a loss of an opportunity for larger supportive impact and possibly a lasting collegial relationship. It cannot be overemphasized: foundations' role is not simply to hand out money. More of their personnel need to be aware of that and encouraged to act on it.

Foundations have a stake in creating cultures of experimentation. Most research and creative development are inherently risky. Foundations are right to support those who try; their results are worth celebrating, even when they fail, as they often do. It is necessary to tolerate failure in a culture that wants to encourage learning and innovation. Experiments lead to new strategic direction and, sometimes, to unanticipated success. Many foundations appear to have forgotten what earned them recognition in former times: a culture that encouraged experimentation, repeated efforts, action, and learning. A foundation that lacks the leadership and staff to recognize risk taking as essential to significant achievement is not likely to bet on, or even recognize, the kinds of individuals who can make breakthroughs or significant progress on a problem. As Robert Merton reminded us, the immaculate-appearing research paper obscures what makes for a creative inquiry: "intuitive leaps, false starts, mistakes, loose ends, and happy accidents." That does not play well in the predominant culture of success.

There is, as John Sawyer wrote, "a need for demystification and for self-scrutiny in how programs are projected and applicants are treated. Beyond what any applicant has a right to expect—courtesy, candor, promptness of reply—most fields would be better served if foundation staffs and boards recognized that best knowledge can almost always be found 'out there.' "

Foundations have a way to go to meet those standards.